Finding Our She-Compass

Finding Our She-Compass

15 Life Lessons For Women Voyaging toward Restoration, Reconstruction, and Renewal

CONCEPT, STORIES, AND ANECDOTES BY HELEN OWENS

DEVELOPED AND EDITED BY JO OWENS

ISBN-13: 9781978044739
ISBN-10: 1978044739
Library of Congress Control Number: 2017915795
CreateSpace Independent Publishing Platform
North Charleston, South Carolina

Acknowledgements

Special thanks to our seafaring sister Charlotte Ziems, whose uncompromising commitment to sisterhood helped make this book possible.

Contents

Introduction

"Love is the compass of life."

-- PECKEROY

If it's true we are all the captains of our own ships, then my truth is that I've spent my life as the co-captain of a vessel of women circumnavigating the world on pilgrimages to self-discovery. Relying on my soul's compass of kindness, compassion, empathy, and trust, I've been on a voyage through the hearts and minds of many incredibly precious creatures. Together, we've tirelessly sailed the world's torrential seas to find answers to life's questions, gaining a great love for one another along the way.

In the beginning, we were all rugged pirates searching for the same treasure. I was a veteran hair-loss and hair-replacement expert that guided my fair maidens in wars against the physical and mental challenges of going bald in a world where our hair is inextricably linked to our femininity, dignity, and ultimately, our self-worth. I brought my years of award-winning hands-on experience, my knowledgebase of medical resources, and countless client stories of survival and success to the table to let my ladies know I truly understood their journey. I began losing my hair as a child and knew all too well the impact that losing our crowning glory could have on one's self-esteem.

But as our time together grew, I came to realize that I was filling a void in the souls of these women. I became a springboard to self-exploration for women in transition, a comforter through their personal trials, and a protector of their biggest secrets and fears. It is a badge of honor I wear proudly, as I know this unique soul-trait is a gift from God. It's been 30 years and counting, and I still marvel at the opportunity to witness the triumph of spirit these women undergo when regaining all of who they are.

I bonded with women from every lifestyle and every level of society, women who are private citizens and public figures; together we found common ground in helping one another strengthen our hearts and spirits, until each of us was strong enough to fully become the beautiful goddesses we were meant to be. For these women, I wasn't just their stylist—I became, in their words, their best friend. I'm so fortunate that my life's work has afforded me the opportunity to both exercise my philosophical perspective about the world and its people and share with thousands of women my understanding of the intricacies of benevolence.

It is because of the great love I have developed for women and for humanity that I am hopeful we can all learn to develop for ourselves and each other a legitimate love, one that is steeped in protection of the hearts and spirits of others, without personal objectives or agendas.

To that end, I hope that by sharing a few of my experiences, I can create a framework for what we can do to be better to ourselves and others—after all, I'm a firm believer that a borrowed lesson is always better than a bought one. The stories included in the following pages are based on composites of many women I've encountered and loved, and whose journeys toward finding their innate, distinct identities I was fortunate to be a part of. I've created pseudonyms in place of their real names, and combined selected events, conversations, and tales from their individual adventures to create blended narratives.

As you read their stories, my hope is that they can show by example that we can all use our thoughts and actions to positively influence the emotional well-being of everyone around us. I hope these intimate stories inspire each of us to hone and honor our personal power, raise our awareness of the subtleties required to be an effective participant in life, and strengthen our ever-evolving ability to experience perfect love in this lifetime. Relationships are often the gateway to discovering our best selves; my hope is to show through my relationships with these amazing women how we can use our very lives to fulfill completely ourselves and others.

One

How I Became a Captain

*"I am not afraid of storms for I am
learning how to sail my ship."*

– Louisa May Alcott

*M*y foray into being a leader and protector for women on the path to self-discovery began as a child; I realized early on that I had an innate ability to show women their value just by being present in their lives.

I found my strength while growing up in San Francisco. Prior to our move to public housing, my fondest memories are of being with my mother, father, and five siblings in the Lakeview, Avenues, and bordering neighborhoods of the Haight-Ashbury/Fillmore districts. Even though I had the opportunity to grow up in one of the most progressive cities in the country, I still understood as a little African-American girl in America during the mid-sixties and early seventies that my parents would have to work very hard to achieve even the smallest amount of prosperity.

Like many African-American families before them, my parents were a part of the Great Migration from the South, packing up their kids and journeying to big cities where labor work was plentiful and could offer more opportunities for a better life. My parents took the train from New Orleans when I was still a baby, heading to San Francisco where my dad went to work painting some of the city's greatest historical landmarks, including the famous "Painted Ladies" Victorian homes. He worked hard, taking any and all painting jobs he could find to earn money. My mother once shared with me that Dad convinced the landlord to waive the first month of rent in exchange for painting the entire interior and exterior of the seven-room Victorian on Ellis Street where they first lived.

I remember vividly how proud I was of Dad's relationship with his employer Sammy. They were boss and subordinate, but they also shared a mutual respect. Sammy was a white man who made sure my father had plenty of work to help feed his family, and that relationship was a clear contrast to the segregated environments of Louisiana my parents had just left. My mother always spoke highly of Sammy, and the fact that he cared greatly for my Dad was always acknowledged in our home. My mother was especially fond of the metal lunch box and matching thermostat Sammy gave my Dad as a welcome gift for joining his team. Sammy had the centers of its symbolic front-metal clasps carefully etched with my Dad's initials, and my mother filled it daily with coffee and fried-bologna sandwiches, my Dad's favorite. The lunchbox was special to us all, because it was Sammy's way of letting my Dad know he was both a welcomed colleague and a friend.

My mother and father were hip San Franciscans and big fans of rhythm and blues. They had huge record collections of artists like Bobby Blue Bland, Wilson Pickett, and my father's personal favorite, Sam Cook. Sometimes after Dad came home from work they'd go out for the evening; Dad had a little singing gig at one of the local bars, and on the occasions that my mother could get our neighbor to watch us for the evening, she would step out with her girlfriends and meet up with my father. I'd watch as my mother transformed from a housewife in a robe and hair curlers into a goddess in beautiful high heels and hip leisure suits. She would style her wigs and wig pieces to cover the alopecia diagnosis I would eventually inherit into fashionable beehives, flips, and afros. She'd carefully apply foundation from her Posner or Flori Roberts compacts, add a touch of color from the blue, sample-lipstick box she collected from the Avon lady, then prance out the door proud as a peacock. I remember a lot of love in my household at that time.

Of all my siblings, I've been told all my life I was most like my father. I have fond childhood memories of him taking me to the donut shop every morning before he went to work—he'd pick me up, put me in the seat beside him, and make it a point to ask the shopkeeper to make sure my glazed donut was fresh out of the fryer.

I guess some part of me even then wanted to be an entrepreneur, because as a five-year-old I was devising ways to make money to help my parents. Together, my father and I came up with "the donut-house shuffle." Dad would lift me onto the table where we were sitting, and I would tap dance like Shirley Temple, smiling proudly in my lace-ruffled ankle socks, patent-leather black buckle-shoes and short pink dress with matching yarn-ribbons tied around the short ponytail in my hair. People in the booths would "ooh" and "ahh" and tell Dad what a beautiful daughter he had while they'd drop a few nickels and quarters on the tables for me.

By the end of the day I'd have anywhere from 5 to 10 dollars saved. For a little girl like me, it was like winning the lottery—it felt great to have money in my pocket for Boston Baked Beans, Red Hots, and Scooter Pies, and to have that priceless time with Dad. Afterward, Dad and I would trek down to Ocean Beach, which was only a few miles from the donut shop. We were greeted at the entrance by Laughing Sal, a large female puppet encased in glass, with a red-lipped grin and accompanying gapped-tooth smile. We'd ride the carousel first; my favorite place to sit was always in the carriage. Two colorfully painted horses flanked it, each with a blend of purple, red, and yellow on their pastel saddles, and their pearl painted lips glistened in the sun as they rode up and down on their electric poles. I laughed with pure, unadulterated joy, and celebrated this incredible time in my life.

Our beautiful four-and five-bedroom Victorian homes in Lakeview and Fillmore were the manifestation of the high hopes for prosperity my parents had. My mother insisted that my "princess room," as one of my siblings called it, had loads of stuffed animals and a beautiful pink canopy bed.

Uncharted Waters

It's when my parents split that things began to change. I was seven years old. I watched as both my parents made plans to walk away from life together as they knew it.

The first thing to go was the home they shared. My father moved to a tiny studio apartment in the Tenderloin, and my mother moved with her six children to public housing in Hunter's Point. To say this was a difficult time for my family is putting it lightly—we all mourned the physical breakup of our family, and my siblings and I hated that the father we loved and cherished couldn't live with us under the same roof. Most challenging was that neither of my parents no longer had each other for financial support; the dreams they'd mapped out as a married couple were now dissolved. We all tried to settle in and manage our new life—for my siblings and I, shuffling back and forth between two small apartments several days a week was the new normal, and the sooner we put behind us our happy memories of living together, the easier the transition would be.

Accepting that she'd have to go back to work after years of being a stay-at-home mom was no easy feat for my mother. She bravely exchanged her housecoat and slippers for a waitressing apron at a famous sports bar called Lefty O'Doul's. Its claim to fame was that it was founded by the San Francisco pitcher and outfielder of the same name, who was also a mentor and close friend of MLB Hall-of-Famer Joe DiMaggio, the 1930s-1940s all-star MVP of the world-champion New York Yankees. My mother said that by the time she'd arrived, Lefty's had been enshrined as the go-to sports bar in San Francisco—she had vivid memories of frequent visits from Joe DiMaggio and his wife, the iconic Marilyn Monroe, breezing in for a meal whenever they were in town, and the bar's popularity helped put more tips in her pocket.

My mother had her share of brushes with plenty of celebrities while working there. Her clearest memories are of seeing NBA Hall-of-Famers and Golden State Warriors legends Wilt Chamberlain and Nate Thurmond, both of whom couldn't get enough of the barbeque. The Whispers would come in for "breakfast and burgers" when they were in town, and San Francisco Giants MLB Hall-of-Famer Willie McCovey, who used to "order from the line" was kind to the staff with each short visit. I watched as my mother settled into her breadwinner role, and was proud to see her "keep on trucking" without her husband or his much-needed salary.

Two

SUBMERGED IN THE BERMUDA TRIANGLE

"If loving you is wrong, I don't want to be right."

— LUTHER INGRAM

T hough her days at work were long and often arduous, my mother received some brief respite from her distressed life when she'd see her regular customers. These were the patrons who knew my mother was a struggling single parent living in public housing, so when she'd smile at them when topping their coffee cups, or ensured their orders were made just right, they expressed their appreciation in large tips—my mother's "regulars" did what they could to make sure she had enough money to feed her children at the end of her shifts.

From the time my mother and father separated, my mother focused solely on taking care of herself and her children. Given this, I never imagined she'd ever again have an interest in dating. But if she did, I always thought it would be a customer that would catch her eye—they all liked her so much that it seemed like a natural progression. Particularly Jim, a nice white man who always left a solid one-hundred-dollar bill for my mother. As it turned out, the person who did end up drawing my mother's interest wasn't a customer at all.

Smooth Operator

Ralph showed up in our lives about six months after we'd arrived in Hunter's Point. My mother and father were still amicable about family matters, but both fully agreed they were no longer in a marriage. My Dad had a few "lady friends," and my mother seemed content, at least in my seven-year old eyes, to be fine with being single.

So I was surprised when my mother appeared to take an interest in this suave, smooth-talking impeccably dressed man. He coupled close-fitting, wide-lapelled shirts with high-waisted slim slacks that showed off his tall broad shoulders and trim figure. He made sure to have his Stetson fedora tipped ever-so-perfectly to one side over his dark-brown Afro to show off his neatly trimmed sideburns. He made sure his Florsheim wing-tipped shoes were always freshly polished, and never buttoned his superbly-fitting trench coat higher than the middle of his chest—he wanted to be sure his stylish ascot or medallion jewelry peeked out of his neckline at all times. He walked with the gait of a self-assured man who was used to being in control of his environment. As youthful as he tried to appear, Ralph was about 15 years older than my mother.

Ralph, his live-in girlfriend Dorothy, and their son Travis lived around the corner and up the hill, and it wasn't long before one of my brothers and Travis became friends. My brother would spend hours at a time with Travis and Dorothy, excited to play with the kids in his new neighborhood. And with our mother working all the time, it was great for my brother to have the extra company.

One day Ralph decided to walk my brother home—he arrived at our house just as my mother was preparing dinner. He introduced himself and explained that he had been home on a break from his job as a merchant seaman. He thought it best to meet the parent of the child who had been at his house every day for the last week and a half. We thanked him for getting my brother home safely, and asked if he wanted to stay for dinner. He politely declined, saying he had a prior engagement, and we wished him well. We didn't expect to see much more of him, except for those occasions when he dropped by to make sure my brother got home safely from his house.

As time went on, Ralph would pop up about once a month or so on break from his travels abroad. He came back with tales that he thought we'd find interesting, but left out numerous specific details about what he did while at sea. And this time his visits didn't include Travis. I think he was afraid that as close as my brother and Travis were, if Travis got too comfortable at our house, he might accidentally let on that his father had no intention of giving up his live-in girlfriend while he was courting my mother.

Ralph's excuse for always being vague about who he was and what he did with his time was conveniently blamed on his occupation—he claimed his contract with the Navy did not allow him the liberty to disclose too many details, and he was more than happy to provide ambiguous answers if any of us questioned him too closely. The one thing he was honest about was that he was filled with fear anytime he had to work in the South China Sea—he was audibly exposed almost daily to the battle between North and South Vietnam, and the continuous gunfire and bombing made him want to cry like a baby. Knowing that thousands of innocent lives were at risk, he told us it took everything he had to keep doing his job under such duress. I was just a little girl during this time, but I knew when I'd see Ralph's determinedly masculine eyes slightly glaze over and fill with the smallest bit of tears that this part of his job was honestly hard on him. When I would hear adults mention words like "Viet Cong," "Saigon," and "The Draft" I could see by the looks on their faces the great toll this war was exacting on people here at home. I'd only wished Ralph could have been as truthful about himself as he was about the war.

In between asking if we could "parlez-vous francais" and "spreekt u Nederlands"—in any language from countries he'd visited—he'd pat us on our heads, give my mother a quick kiss on the cheek, and unload for us his bag of goodies. For a while it was like having our own private Santa Claus; he'd arrive with a pocket full of money for us and shower my mother with all sorts of gifts. Whether he was lavishing my mom with tickets to Ike and Tina Turner at the Circle Star Theater in San Carlos, taking her to see Sarah Vaughn and Ella Fitzgerald at the Fairmont Hotel in Nob Hill, or pampering her with fancy dinners at the Equinox—an Embarcadero Center restaurant famous for its spinning, three-hundred-sixty-degree view—Ralph made sure our mom was happy. And seeing her happy allowed our family to finally see some relief from the daily grind of hard life. He and my mother's courtship lasted a few more months before he became our stepfather.

Doomed Shipmates

I remember the small wedding at Ralph's brother's house, a comfortable Victorian in the Fillmore. Guests entered the front door into the living room and were greeted by a long table of champagne and a beautiful three-tiered white cake with vanilla frosting. Card tables dotted the room, replacing the chairs and couches that were moved to make room for the event.

On one side of the room was a gorgeous antique fireplace, one of the last remaining architectural pieces from the home's original design. Right above it was a beautiful, gilded mirror, encased in faux gold-leafing. It was through this mirror that I caught the first glimpse of my beautiful mother entering the room. She wore a long-sleeved, A-line floor-length silver colored satin dress that sparkled slightly when the afternoon sun flowing through the floor-to-ceiling windows graced its bodice. It was trimmed with a V-necked, ivory-lace collar that accented her beautiful brown skin and eyes, and the soft fabric lightly wisped around her as she moved.

It had taken her weeks to find this dress. She didn't want to wear white at her second wedding, and in those days finding a non-white wedding dress was next to impossible. Marriage at that time was considered a lifetime commitment—every woman expected to only wear white, one time.

So after searching high and low, and making her way in and out of a myriad of bridal boutiques, my mother finally had to admit to herself that there was likely only one store left in the neighborhood that would carry a non-white special occasion gown. Reluctantly, she made plans to meet up with a co-worker on their lunch break; as they stood outside the Fredrick's of Hollywood store, they each took a deep breath, not sure what they might find when they walked in. Fredrick's was the place to shop for the wedding night, not the wedding day. My mother and her co-worker searched through several racks of form-fitting gowns with way-too-high side slits in every conceivable place.

They sifted and sorted through the garments for what seemed like hours, frustrated that this was their last opportunity to find a dress. Moments later, my mother caught a glimpse of silver peeking out of the racks. She pulled it closer, expecting it to look just like the other risqué gowns with which it was hanging. But this one was perfect—it had just enough flair to be feminine and stylish, and just enough fabric to be delicate and graceful. And the shimmery silver color was so unique it practically jumped off the hanger.

My mother and her co-worker fell in love with this gorgeous gown at first sight, and now I had the chance to see her in it for the first time. I couldn't stop gazing at her; my mother looked like an angel. She coupled this beautiful gown with a matching hat and veil ensemble that adorned her perfectly coiffed hair. I approached her to give her a kiss and hug and could smell the expensive, sweet powdery perfume Ralph had given her as a wedding present. This was my mother's special day, and I was incredibly happy for her.

The first two to three months of my mother's marriage to Ralph was full of contentment. We were happy to be living with this man, who ensured our bills were paid and showered love and affection on my mother and her children. For a while, it seemed everyone was doing well. It didn't take long for all of us to realize Ralph was the quintessential Jekyll and Hyde.

Drinks with the Crew

The first glimpse I had of the man Ralph truly was became apparent after he returned home from working in the Philippines. He came back with his usual stories, only this time, the first thing he did was pour himself a glass of Vodka and orange juice. I was only about nine and a half, but I knew this mixture was much more potent than the Kool-Aid we kids drank daily or the occasional Coca Cola we'd get from the corner store. A day would not go by for the next few months that I wouldn't catch Ralph pouring himself a swig of his "joy juice" several times a day.

The "parties" started shortly thereafter. Luckily it was my mother's rule that adults needed time alone to discuss "grown folks business," so none of us were allowed in the living room while the parties were taking place. Of course, that didn't mean we didn't sneak out of our rooms to watch from the stairway landing what was going on.

Ralph would invite his best friend Wayne, who lived with his wife Juanita in the building across from us, over for drinks on weekends. He and Ralph were close in age, but Wayne looked much older. He was about 40 pounds overweight, and years of smoking, coupled with the stress of trying to survive life in the ghetto, had put heavy premature wrinkles in his forehead. Being able to party with Ralph on his off-days was the highlight of Wayne's week, and he was so excited to have a "night out" that he doused himself in what smelled like an entire bottle of Aqua Velva aftershave.

Ralph would convince my mother he and Wayne were just going to "party a little," and that Wayne and Juanita's visit would last only a couple hours so my mother and her children could get to bed at a reasonable time. My mother was not a heavy drinker by any means and only very occasionally would sample a glass of wine or indulge in a tiny bit of Kahlua to satisfy her sweet tooth. In the beginning, I think she figured it was easier to let Ralph spend a few hours blowing off steam with a drink or two than to disallow it altogether and possibly end up in an argument. So she reluctantly went along. And on the bright side, she figured, it would give her a chance to get to know Juanita a little better.

It turned out both Juanita and Wayne caused my mother's household more trouble than the compromise was worth. As soon as Wayne hit the door, he'd make a beeline for the gin Ralph stored in the cupboard, sometimes drinking it straight or mixing it with a bottle of juice he'd grabbed from my mother's refrigerator.

And Juanita was no better, though she tried at first to convince everyone in the room she was. After being invited in she'd slowly sashay into the living area and speak to my mother in what sounded like some kind of rehearsed mid-Atlantic accent she'd borrowed from starlets like Katherine Hepburn or Joan Crawford. She'd slowly lower herself onto the sofa, making sure not to let too much leg peek out of her knee-length polyester skirt. Her long legs would be perfectly crossed in front of her and her speech was articulate and rhythmic. Her matching hat and jacket proved she'd spent some hours trying to one-up anything my mother might have worn for the evening. Juanita was the picture of lady-like perfection. That is, until she'd reach coyly into her purse for that silver-plated decorative flask that contained what she secretly called her "moonshine-apple-wine."

At first, as she sipped smartly from that silver container, Juanita gave zero indication she was imbibing 80-proof alcohol. But with every sip she would get closer to exchanging her modesty for completely uninhibited behavior. It wasn't long before she'd slip from her proper, stiff-backed, crossed-leg ladylike position into the spread-legged, flailing-armed, slurred-speech alcoholic she truly was. And it didn't stop there; once Juanita was sufficiently inebriated, her truest colors would begin to show.

Her speech, no longer sprinkled with light laughter and the occasional "dahling," after every comment, now gave way to straight-out profanity directed at Wayne and illicit, sexual innuendo directed at Ralph. Thank goodness my brothers weren't in the room—she might have propositioned them next!

She'd get up slowly and head over to the mahogany-framed hi-fi stereo console that was designed to look like a fine piece of living room furniture. She'd first make sure her favorite songs by Al Green or Millie Jackson were spinning on the record player, then she'd reach into the console center to turn up the volume so loudly people blocks away could hear. She'd gyrate back and forth with her drink firmly in hand, singing the lyrics in her tone-deaf voice. Soon enough, she'd start looking in Wayne's direction using words from the music to mock him. Juanita made no bones about the fact that Wayne was a no-show in the bedroom and she used her "parties" to tell the world what she thought about Wayne's lack of affection toward her.

"You motherfucker! You think you can get away with going to work all day and not taking care of me when you get home? Motherfucker I'll get it anywhere I can, and ain't a damn thing you can do about it!" That's when she'd lay eyes on Ralph.

"Come over here baby and give mama some sugar," she'd coo across the room to a just-starting-to-get-buzzed Ralph, who even in his tipsy state knew my mother was eyeing him to see how he'd respond to Juanita's inappropriate behavior. "Now, Miss Juanita," he'd say, "go on wit' yo'self now. You and Wayne always havin' problems but ya'll gonna be alright." No matter how unacceptable Juanita's behavior became, Ralph always had a way of making sure he was in the safe zone with my mother.

Smart though Ralph's comments were, they weren't the response Juanita was looking for. She wanted attention and was determined to get it. She'd sink further down into the sofa, then deliberately spread her legs as wide as she could to ensure everyone in the room knew she wasn't wearing underwear. She'd sit wide-legged for a few minutes to make sure everyone could get a good look, then touch herself with one hand while she held tightly onto her drink with the other. In between expletives, she'd holler as loud as she could to anyone who'd listen. "This is the good stuff baby! Ain't nobody got pussy like mine!"

My mother would look at her in horror, and do everything she could to get Ralph to get these two the hell out of her house. Of course, Ralph by now was in his own liquored-up state and had no plans to end the party early.

Some days Juanita would give up trying to solicit sex from Ralph, or anyone for that matter. She would arrive so frustrated with Wayne that it was easier just to spend the evening embarrassing him.

Of all the physical issues Wayne had with his body, the one secret he tried very hard to keep was the fact that he was bald. I was very sympathetic toward Wayne's decision to keep his hair condition private—I was a child with a confirmed hair loss condition and the kid of a mother who wore incredibly fashionable wigs. But when I laid eyes on Wayne for the first time, I struggled to understand how he could keep his baldness a secret. He had a collection of toupees that were truly some of the most poorly designed, ill-fitting hairpieces I'd ever seen. And Juanita made it a point to capitalize on this issue.

On the days that she was feeling particularly resentful toward Wayne, Juanita would wait until he was so intoxicated that he couldn't properly defend himself. Then she'd rip his toupee right off his head and run around the room with it, shaking it at him and calling him all kinds of names. For a little girl who knew what it felt like to have kids tease her about "the bald disease," this was more than I could take. This kind of meanness these "grown folks" had for each other, whether they were drunk or not, just wasn't acceptable to me.

Though it still baffles me to this day how she did it, somehow my mother withstood Ralph's "parties" along with his own alcoholic behavior for the next several years. I think knowing he would be gone for six to nine months at a time helped tremendously; this gave her the time and space she needed to stay focused on working and keeping her kids safe. For the most part, she was able to do just that, but there would be one event during that period that would test my mother's—and my family's—strength to no end.

Lightning on the Sea

Adjusting to life as a child of separated parents wasn't easy, but one thing I was determined to do was be a part of both my mother's and father's lives. While my mother tried to navigate her chaotic marriage to Ralph, my siblings and I visited our Dad as often as we could. My Dad made it clear to us that even though he was no longer living with us, he was still our father and nothing could change that.

We split our days between two of the people we loved the most—though my mother often griped about the amount of time we'd spend away from our home with her, she did take comfort in knowing that her children were with their father. The two of them may have had their differences, but my siblings and I loved our Dad, and we did our best to make sure he knew it.

So when my mother received a call one evening from my aunt saying our Dad had passed in his sleep, alone in his apartment with Joe Simon's "Drowning in the Sea of Love" still spinning on the record player, we were devastated beyond belief. Our family was already enduring the emotional and financial challenges of living without Dad, but losing permanently one of our parental anchors was a hardship for which none of us were prepared.

I was only 11 years old, but I had to quickly learn what it meant to keep pushing forward in the face of inexplicable grief. I was faced with the realization that I would never again hear Dad call my name, or hear him tell me in his own voice how much he loved me. He was gone, and my world was forever changed. The only thing left to cling to were my fond memories of him. I could hold tight to visions of cooking fried bananas sprinkled with sugar in his small kitchen. I would forever cherish the hours of fighting I did with my siblings about whether "Gilligan's Island" or "Bewitched" would win out as the dinnertime entertainment on Dad's small black-and-white Zenith TV. I could see clearly the phone calls our mother would make to Dad's apartment "on a school night," begging him not to keep us up past our bedtime.

The person who was most like me had left, and I had to learn to keep my head up and power through life in the face of tragedy. I was already a child growing up dodging the pimps, prostitutes, and drug dealers that peppered the streets of Hunter's Point, but not having my father around to share my life experience made it harder. I longed to take trips to the Tenderloin to talk one-on-one with my Dad, just like we did when I was a kid at the donut shop. I missed that special father-daughter time, and tried to live as best I could knowing I would never get it back. So I decided at the age of 15, when I learned I was pregnant, that this child would give me the chance to have the unconditional love I missed from my Dad. Though I knew being a teenage mother would be one of the biggest challenges I would face in my life, I looked forward to the genuine love and affection that comes only from a child—I wanted someone to need me the way I needed them.

A Maiden's Voyage

Growing up without my Dad and watching my mom struggle to keep a roof over our heads gave me a fierce determination to overcome the challenges life would throw my way—even as a teenager, I knew getting free of the projects and having the life I wanted would require plenty of strong will and perseverance.

My plan was to keep my pregnancy private until delivery time, then leave home, have the baby on my own, and begin my new life with my child. So with the help of baggy sweatshirts and oversized sweatpants, I kept my pregnancy hidden as long as possible—until the prying eyes of a visiting aunt noticed the severe swelling around my belly.

When my mother learned about the baby, she didn't have the reaction I thought she would. I was sure she'd be overcome with sadness and disappointment that her daughter was about to become a teenage mother. But I think the struggles our family was enduring helped my mother empathize with the emotions surrounding my pregnancy—she understood very well what it felt like to have a child's unconditional love, and also understood that I needed this in my life at that time. We don't get "do-overs" in life, and hindsight is always twenty-twenty—if I knew then what I know now, I would definitely have waited to have children. But I'm grateful for the love my son—and also my daughter Isabel, who would follow just after I turned 17—gave me. They were my hope for the future, and I needed all the hope I could get.

My mother also made it clear to me that I was welcome to stay with her as long as I felt I needed to. As mentally prepared as I was to leave, I knew I would need time to adjust to life with my child, so I was very thankful for her offer. And it didn't take long for my son's grandmother to fall in love with my child—my mother was filled with pure joy each time she looked at my baby. Aaron was the apple of both her and Ralph's eye, and their "Pooh-Bear," as they called him, was given all the love and attention they could muster. My mother and Ralph even offered to adopt my baby so I would have the opportunity to finish school and not have the hardship of trying to raise a baby as a teenager, though that was a burden I simply could not allow them to carry.

I also believe my mother understood intrinsically that motherhood is a unique experience for each person. She, too, at one time agonized over a pregnancy that could have compromised her and her baby's life. What she needed most at that time from family and friends was the very thing she gave me—physical and emotional support, as she faced one of the most difficult decisions of her life. Doctors confirmed early in my mother's pregnancy that she was to become the mother of a blind and limbless child—I can only image the emotional, physical, and financial challenges this would have placed on a young mother already struggling to make it in this world with the few resources she had. Thankfully the recent passage of Roe v. Wade made it possible for my mother to become one of the first women in her generation to benefit from being able to choose whether to have a child for which she was ill-prepared.

Another reason my mother understood that I—not his grandparents—wanted to be the one to raise Aaron, was because she'd also had a brush with losing her children. In the days when Ralph and my mother were just getting to know each other, they treated themselves to a few hours at a New Year's Eve Party, promising themselves and their oldest son, who would be left "in charge" while they were gone, that they'd be home shortly after midnight. For us younger kids, it was just another night, and we were in our pajamas and ready for bed by 10:00 pm.

I don't remember falling into the very heavy sleep I was in when I heard one of my siblings calling my name from outside my bedroom window. Thankfully my oldest brother had chosen to disobey our mother that night and sneak out for about an hour just before midnight. It was from the street as he made his way home that he watched our family home burning in a blazing fire, with his five siblings trapped inside. Within minutes, he had managed to get indoors, fan the flames, and wake one of my younger brothers, who ran outside and then proceeded to alert me. "Helen! The house is on fire! Wake up!"

My younger brother told me later he screamed at the very top of his lungs for a good five minutes before he could rouse me, but when I awoke and saw black smoke coming from my other siblings' bedrooms, I bolted into action. I hit the floor and "dropped and rolled" just like I was taught in grade school, crawling under the smoke to get to their rooms. I will never forget the fear overwhelming me when I couldn't get them to wake up, scared-to-death they had already passed from smoke inhalation. I damn-near threw another of my brothers off the bed before he awoke, and he helped me get the rest of our siblings out. Children are resilient and fearless; as an adult, I don't know how we all survived jumping from our second-floor windows to safety, but we did it without any thought of the consequences. All we could focus on was getting out of that building.

It's only after I became a mother that I understood the paralyzing fear that struck my own mother when one of the party guests told her that her house was on fire. She told me that when she found my oldest brother, she begged him to tell her where her children were, and his answer still resonated with her years later. "Momma, they're all here. I know, because I counted them." My 13-year-old brother was a hero to us all. In all the terror he was experiencing, he made sure he and his siblings were safe and wouldn't give up until he could account for every one of them.

The one devastating loss we all experienced was losing our two four-legged family members, dogs we called Prince and Storm. We learned later that Prince had died of smoke inhalation while hiding under my mother's bed. He saw the flames early on, and was so fearful that he'd wedged himself into a corner and never came out. Storm's fate was worse—when we later found his charred body, we'd realized he'd been directly engulfed by the heat of the flames. Our sorrow was met with only a small amount of relief upon learning from our mother that our beloved animals were now with God, in Doggie Heaven. As we all gathered together, hugging one another, we breathed a collective sigh of relief, wrapping ourselves in blankets from the Red Cross. By the grace of God, we had all survived, with the greatest injuries among us sprained ankles and bruised arms and legs.

Like many families in public housing, we had to fight daily not to let the hardships in our lives become a precursor to our future—generations of families had lived and died in the projects, and if we wanted to be the family that survived outside the walls of Hunter's Point, we'd have to find a way to keep alive our parents' hopes for their children's successful future. It was up to us to "make it outta here." I held onto that determination, and committed myself to making sure my son and I could carve out our chosen destiny. And it's because of that commitment that I decided within a year of my son being born that it was best for me to leave home.

Three

DROWNING IN THE VORTEX

*"Say I'm gonna turn loose a thousand times a day, how
can I turn loose when I just can't break away?"*

— CANDI STANTON

In the years I lived with my mother and her husband, I tried hard to understand what about Ralph made my mother want to remain in his life. Even as a child, I sensed Ralph was not what he appeared, and as his drinking escalated I watched him transform into the monster I knew him to truly be. By now I was well prepared for the chaos Ralph would bring each time he'd return home—he'd get drunk, threaten to "deal later" with my mother, and my mother would find a way to make excuses for his torrid behavior. I wondered if there would ever come a day when my mother would choose to protect herself instead of protecting him.

Each day I watched my mother try to hold onto what little bit of her marriage to Ralph she had left. Her days were the same—she'd go to work, then come home to dote on her kids and grandchild, happy to have as much time away from Ralph as possible. But the last straw came sooner than I expected, and that's when I took my baby and left her house.

It was the end of a long week; by now, I had been working full time for just over a year, having made the decision to leave school at 16 so I could feed my son and offer whatever was left to my mother. I'd been home for a few hours and was finally getting to bed after getting my son to sleep.

Just as I was starting to fall asleep I heard sounds coming from my mother's room—first a loud thump, then what sounded like a muffled cry. I jumped up and ran to my bedroom door, slowly cracking it open so I could decipher what I was hearing. The cries became louder, and when I realized the cries were coming from my mother, I swung open my door and ran down the hallway to her bedroom. As I got closer, I could hear Ralph admonishing my mother to "keep quiet so the kids couldn't hear." At that moment I knew he was over-powering her and that my mother's safety was severely in jeopardy. I banged on my mother's bedroom door so hard I watched the wood indent every time my fist made contact.

I called out to my mother, "I'm gonna break this door down if you don't come out! I don't know what the hell is going on in there, but I do know some-body better answer this door right now!" I think if Ralph hadn't heard some of the stories my siblings told about me—that I never rushed to fight, but had been seen knocking out my fair share of assholes wanting to try getting a piece of me—then he wouldn't have let my mother come to the door. Ralph knew better than to try my patience.

My mother came to the door and slowly opened it. She had covered her-self with her robe but I knew she was only partially clothed underneath. That damned Ralph sat on the corner of the bed, trying his best not to make eye contact with me as I peeked into the bedroom. "Smart move, man," I thought to myself. "Because if you think I'm gonna put up with any of what you tried to give my mother, you'll be one dead son-of-a-bitch when I get through with you."

My mother waved me back into the hallway and slowly came out of her bedroom. She put her arm around me and walked me back to my room. I told her this was it—that it was time for her to leave Ralph so she could put an end to his behavior. I pretended not to know what had happened to her, but once I saw Ralph's face I figured out exactly what was going on. The loud thump I heard was him jumping on top of her while she was asleep. And her cries were that of a woman who knew she was about to be violated in the worst way. I wanted to kill that asshole—it took everything I had to let my rational mind take over instead.

My mother sat down with me on my bed. I told her there was no excuse for being treated this way and begged her to leave this man. She refused, saying he was overall a good man to her and the kids and she still wanted to be his wife. I was dumbfounded by her response but knew there was nothing more I could do. This man that my mother claimed loved her had just tried to rape her and I could only imagine how many other times this had happened. Whether I agreed with it or not, this was the life that my mother believed was best for her. I found it ironic that my mother had no trouble separating from my Dad, a man that was kind to her and was the devoted father of her children. But when it came to Ralph she didn't see separation as an option. I knew it was time for me to make a life separate from this violence, even if that meant I'd have to leave my mother to her own choices.

I pulled out my suitcase as my mother watched, both of us knowing we had come to an impasse. She was prepared to stay in this abusive relationship and there was no way I would tolerate another day of violence after what I'd just witnessed. I slowly began organizing my things, and as I did so, pressed my mother for more information about her relationship with Ralph. That's when she revealed that Ralph began hitting her as early as a month into their marriage. I wasn't surprised that I didn't know this—Ralph knew better than to hit our mother in front of us. He might have been crazy, but he wasn't stupid—he knew full well that my siblings and I would have torn him into a million pieces if we'd seen him hurt even a single hair on our mother's head. And since our father was alive for the first several years of their marriage, Ralph knew better than to let our Dad get word of anyone laying a hand our mother.

My mother told me that at first, she endured the attacks, because as a new wife her only goal at that time was to do everything she could to keep her marriage intact. But as her children got older she started hitting back, and from that point on she would let Ralph have it every time he hit her. Most times he was drunk, and she was sure to use his intoxication as the opportunity to go straight upside his head whenever she needed to.

I'm sure my mother told me this in an attempt to lessen my intense rage, but in a way it only made me angrier—I couldn't believe I was hearing my mother rationalize being hit by her husband, as if "going upside his head" made the whole thing okay. As usual she was defending his behavior instead of tending to her own well-being.

I couldn't imagine being hit once, much less several times over several years. I'd seen with my own eyes Ralph abusing my mother and it was time for me to find another place to raise my child. If only Dad were here, I thought to myself. That damned Ralph wouldn't stand a chance.

My mother sat quietly on my bed and stared at the floor as I folded socks and pulled jeans and blouses from my dresser drawers. She knew it would be just a matter of time before I let my siblings know what I'd seen. And when they did learn what kind of treatment our mother was enduring, they, too, tried to help her understand she didn't have to tolerate Ralph's behavior. But inevitably, their pleas fell on deaf ears. Soon they tired of watching my mother make excuses for Ralph, and like me, all left home as soon as they could.

My mother also admitted that night that she knew about Dorothy. She found out about her roughly a year after she and Ralph were married. While out running errands, my mother discovered Ralph and Dorothy together sitting on a playground bench watching Travis play on the jungle gym. When she bum-rushed them and demanded to know who Dorothy was, Ralph tried to calm my visibly upset mother, quietly explaining Dorothy was his half-sister visiting from Chicago. My mother let it go for the time being but told him she would talk to him about this at home. Convinced Ralph was lying, she politely acknowledged Dorothy and made her way to her next destination. Of course, Ralph would later let on that "his sister" was really his girlfriend. Though they had split up before he and my mother married, Ralph had been living off and on with Dorothy for years. On the days he'd tell my mother he was going back to work, he'd sometimes spend days or even weeks camped out with Dorothy before returning to his job at sea. My mother figured out soon after that Dorothy was just one of several women still in Ralph's life—he also had another common-law wife who lived in the Philippines.

I felt a sense of sadness overcome me as I packed my bag—my mother was more lost than I imagined. Not only was she living with a man who had her convinced that being hit was a natural part of their relationship, she also settled long ago for being yet another woman in Ralph's life instead of demanding the respect due to a wife. As I finished packing and prepared to gather up my son's things, I could only pray that one day my mother would realize she was so much more than the life she was choosing to live.

Lesson One: Unload Excess Baggage

What I realized at that moment was that I could not let my mother's choices shape my future—if I was going to be the captain of my own ship I needed to believe in my own personal power and never compromise who I was.

I loved my mother, and I knew the best way to honor that love was to rise above what life expected of her and that of her daughter. My mother came of age in a segregated world that taught African American children their brown skin made them less valuable than others. And like many young girls of her generation, Black and White, she was raised in a world where marrying and having children was what really turned little girls into grown women—being a wife and mother was the definition of femininity, even if that relationship compromised a woman's health and safety. I was a Black teenage mother from a poor family, which according to statistics meant I was destined to raise my child on welfare and remain in public housing for life. Both my mother and I were written off before we had a chance, but I knew even as a young woman that surviving this life meant choosing to be a victor rather than a victim. I was already saddled with plenty of baggage, but I knew in my heart and soul that it was up to me not to carry this load into the next stage of my life.

My mother's choices understandably shaped her experiences, but I knew she wanted more for her children than life in the mean streets of Hunter's Point. Even in the midst of her own turmoil, she tried hard to remind us that "you may live in the ghetto, but the ghetto doesn't have to live in you." My mother wanted her children to survive on their own even if she couldn't bring herself to exhibit that same behavior. In my mind I had created the character of my mother to be strong and formidable, not a dependent needing to be cared for. I envisioned her as a great leader, a woman who let it be known that it was her way or the highway, and that anyone who even thought about taking another road would have to drive through her first. But the reality was my mother was so co-dependent on the life she had with Ralph that even her deep-seated pain from the way he treated her wasn't enough to make her walk away.

It would take years for my mother to gain the courage to leave, but my siblings and I were well into adulthood by that time. I only wished my mother had learned much earlier in life to be the keeper of her own soul. For years,

Ralph had been her keeper. Then my siblings and I were her keeper, protecting her from her own poor choices. Finally, her inability to recognize her own power kept her from living a life where she always came first. It seemed something or someone was always keeping her from being her best self.

Difficult as these times were, I'm grateful for my life with my mother. I may have been born into this world with the capacity to be strong and determined, but I also believe my determination was enhanced because I saw how committed my mother was to survive. More to the point, I watched how difficult it was for her to believe she counted in a world that taught her she didn't. I wanted so badly to see my mother be the captain of her own ship, the compass of her own soul, and the commander of her own journey.

I can easily see my mother's life in so many of the women I meet. Some of them have access to much more than my mother ever did; many of them have never known poverty, nor have they ever been labeled inferior because of their skin color. But what so many of them have in common is their lack of belief in themselves. It might seem hard to believe in today's world, where countless women like Sheryl Sandberg, Sonya Sotomayor, and Michelle Obama are setting examples for what it means to "lean in." But for women whose souls are in turmoil, the idea that they are relevant, even exceptional, is an idea that remains beyond their grasp.

I've seen directly what happens when a woman can't understand her value or who she is. In every case, it's like watching an eagle that once soared above the highest mountains suddenly tuck its wings and freefall to Earth. I remind my ladies that holding onto useless baggage of any kind—meaningless relationships, dissatisfying careers, unhappy life choices—comes with a hefty price. I want them instead to be true to their essence and forever remain commanders-in-chief of their own souls. Each of us has a responsibility to know and own ourselves so that we can be the full human beings that we are intended to be. When we take the time to remember that we must always come first, we lift ourselves to our highest consciousness and rise to our greatest potential.

Four

Friendship's Treacherous Waters

"A man that hath friends must shew himself friendly."

— PROVERBS 18:24

One of the earliest lessons I learned in life is that true love has zero conditions. I've been a Fur Mom for years, relishing all the love my dogs, rabbits, cats, and birds have showered upon me in my happiest and darkest times. What I am most grateful for is witnessing how each of these animals show love and the great respect they demonstrate for each other.

Rudy the house cat would sit quietly in the corner, eyeing Sherman the yellow Labrador out of the corner of his eye as soon as Sherman entered the room. Sherman weighed in at about 90 to 100 pounds any given day, and Rudy knew once they were in the same room together he would have to mentally prepare himself for Sherman's excitement and adulation.

Sherman would roll on the floor in front of Rudy and then jab Rudy with his paw—Rudy would shoot Sherman a look of irritation and scrunch closer into a corner, trying to make his body somehow disappear from the burly, sloppy-kissing dog who simply wanted to love him until he couldn't see straight. Sherman's enthusiasm for his cat-brother never waned, even when Rudy once clawed Sherman's nose so strongly that Sherman let out a soft yelp.

To Sherman, Rudy was his playmate, his pack member, his family. Sherman didn't care how irritated Rudy became; he was always going to show Rudy he loved him. I could watch these two exchange love-taps for hours—this was real love, and it filled my heart with complete joy.

No matter what kind of day I was having or what kind of pain I was in, my animals loved me with everything they had; most of all they loved me without expectations, conditions, or restrictions. How I longed to see humans love one another in this way.

I want the next stage of my life to be fulfilled unequivocally with unconditional, legitimate love. I know from experience that love can renew us and reconstruct us, transforming us into the best versions of ourselves. But I also know that love doesn't come easy, particularly from those who are still learning to truly love themselves. I remain hopeful, however, that the remaining years I have left on this planet will attract those whose greatest wish is to love in a way that only empowers themselves and others.

A Lady Is Always the Captain of Her Own Ship

One my earliest relationships was with a woman who came into my life when my children were young. Though as a teenage mother I prided myself on my determination to stand on my own, I still clung to the hope of sharing single-parenthood struggles with another woman. I craved the building up and strengthening we all receive in community with others in similar situations. Though she was 20 years older, Vivian was a best friend to whom I could turn as I undertook the challenges of parenthood and fought for my right to thrive in this world.

Before I knew it, Vivian and I were inseparable. She and I took our children with us everywhere; we rode the city buses all over town with four strollers and four kids strapped to our respective backs. We established ourselves as each other's babysitters when we could, knowing money for day care wasn't an option.

While we toiled away at our jobs, we would dream about the day we could both be truly independent women. Our common goal was to be self-employed so that we would never have to depend on anyone, and so that we could afford to bring up our children in a world that didn't subscribe to the idea that single, poor, Black women could amount to anything.

We were determined to be successful. As an amazing cook, Vivian always wanted to own a thriving, upscale bistro, and I wanted to become the proprietor of a successful hair salon. I looked forward to the day we could celebrate our pact of success. Vivian did what she could to start marketing herself to prospective investors, and I started cleaning houses of wealthy homeowners to pay my way through beauty school. I was so proud to stand with her. We were on our way, and nothing was going to stop us.

About two years into our friendship, as my housecleaning business was just starting to make a profit and Vivian had a solid group of investors and formidable business plan in place, I noticed a change in her. I watched as her once fierce resolve for entrepreneurial success slowly morphed into a fixed obsession with becoming the arm-candy of powerful men.

Vivian was stunningly beautiful; already approaching 40, her looks were so close to perfect that she appeared to be in her mid-20s. The combination of her piercing green eyes and perfectly sculpted face and body were almost paralyzing. But her looks were never a cause of envy for me—my love was unconditional, and she came first. No amount of men circling her could change the commitment I had to her and our friendship.

I, too, was no stranger to attractiveness—I had been told most of my young life that I was pretty and should consider modeling. To this day my mother tells me how irritated she became when photographers on the San Francisco streets stopped her and demanded to take pictures of her child. But I knew even at that point in life, being smart and owning myself was the only real stepping stone to getting free of my life in the projects—I knew relying on physical features alone would be a deterrent to my success. Plus, I had an intimate understanding of what it felt like to be on both sides of pretty. Attractive though I was, I also knew the pain of going bald while trying to raise two kids as a kid myself. I was determined to stay focused on surviving and earning the respect I believed I was due as a human being.

Vivian, on the other hand, focused increasingly on getting a rich man to take care of her. My opportunity to really see her in action would come on the occasions we could get another of our "mommy-network" friends to watch the babies for the evening. I'd watch as a gaggle of men would inflate their chests and flock to their bird of paradise, each hoping Vivian would fall prey to their displays of affection. Every time I'd watch this mating dance, I'd hope Vivian would ignore their charms and instead spread her own wings, let her own plumage shine, and let them know she had the ability to fly like an eagle.

It wasn't long before she started resenting me for coming between her and her life's ambition. "Helen, you're so pretty. You can get these men to pay for everything you need and stop working so hard." The more I refused her offers, the angrier she became. "Look," she'd say to me, "I'm trying to get my life set up so I don't have to worry about my future. I just don't see why you won't go with the flow."

Vivian admitted to me more than once that having a "strong, pretty woman" at her side helped her attract men. Her dates would automatically assume she was just like me—self-assured, intelligent, and eager to lead. But as much as Vivian claimed to love having me as her wing-woman, she was never prepared for the outcome.

Each time it was the same—the men would approach us both, then start up a conversation. I always made it clear I wasn't interested in what I knew they were hoping to get, but what I didn't try to hide was my confidence and strong will. Inevitably, one of Vivian's "rich catches" would invite us to a party at some mansion in the City, and they'd both beg me to come along. I went with her at first to make sure she would make it home safe, but eventually I'd feel like a third wheel.

I have always fully supported a woman's right to exercise her sexuality in any way she sees fit—my beautiful sisters of the world are a blessed assortment of sexual preferences and gender expressions, and I celebrate their right to uniquely express their individual identities. Vivian's sexual self-expression, however, troubled me. It wasn't her desire for casual sex that concerned me—she was a grown woman and had the right to do exactly with her body as she pleased. But it was her use of sexuality solely to target men with little tolerance and respect for independent women that made me uneasy. I knew Vivian to be a proud, free-thinking, self-reliant woman, so watching her transform into a walking blow-up doll devoid of any reasonable level of intellect was more than I could take. If I'd known Vivian's behavior was merely an expression of her sexuality, I would have celebrated her every swing from a chandelier and every "freak flag" she wanted to fly. But what I was witnessing instead was a powerful woman who relinquished her body, mind, and soul simply to garner attention from a man who had no feelings for her and likely even less respect. I was watching my friend alter her entire sense of self, changing from a formidable brick house into a dilapidated shack simply because she believed that not having a man in her life made her incomplete.

Vivian would inevitably end up in doomed relationships with these men, listening to their promises of a life filled with love and luxury. In the beginning she'd hang onto their every word, but in the end the result was always the same. They'd drop her anywhere from a day to six months later, leaving her exactly as they'd found her. Her gravy train came to a screeching halt when she met a powerful Wall Street investment banker. I tried to salvage what was left of the woman I loved as a sister, encouraging her to sock away some of the money he gave her so she'd have a nest egg for herself and her two children. But her Wall Street playboy resented any attempts I made to help Vivian resurrect her personal power—my advice was automatically shot down.

"Why do you rely so much on what that damn Helen says," he'd ask whenever my name came up. "If she told you to jump in front of a San Francisco street car, you'd do it without so much as blinking." Vivian would crumble at his words like a San Francisco hi-rise in a 6.0 earthquake, remind me that the Wall Street playboy was "her man," and that she needed to keep his resources flowing in her direction at any cost. Vivian's loyalties were clear—nothing was going to come between her and "her man," even the fact that the Wall Street playboy was married and had many mistresses at his beck and call.

I learned two things from Vivian's interaction with the Wall Street playboy. First, people (men and women alike) still struggling to understand themselves can be threatened by the strengths of others—the Wall Street playboy's frustration with my expressions of personal power and my attempts at helping Vivian find hers was proof of this. Second, no matter how much I loved Vivian, she simply could not love me the way I needed her to, because she ultimately didn't love herself. It saddened me that Vivian would never understand how important she was as a person, at least not during our friendship.

I slowly began to distance myself from her. To this day, I'm not sure if I hurt more for the loss of a potentially great relationship, or because I knew that by the time this woman realized her worth, the best years of her life would already be behind her.

Sure enough, I did run into her about 10 years later. Her life had turned out exactly as I'd imagined—her looks had faded, she was onto yet another man, and now in her late forties, she was a single mother to five kids instead of two. She did manage to make it in the restaurant business, but as the owner of a corner café instead of the Michelin-certified, upscale restaurant she'd once envisioned. As I looked in those beautiful green eyes that were once only focused on achieving all her dreams, I could only imagine what we could have accomplished together if Vivian had not traded in her ambition to become the property of the opposite sex.

Lesson Two: Protect Your Soul as a Pirate Would Protect Her Treasure

The definition of friendship varies from person to person, but this is one thing I know: we can attain great friendships in our lifetime when we truly understand the essence of who we are. I've tried numerous times to show my female friends and associates by example that our relationships prosper when we are truly in charge of our own souls—when we are firmly planted in our strength and power, we attract those of like mind. As strong as Vivian pretended to be, she chose to sacrifice her essence to attract every eligible bachelor on the planet. I believe we show others how we want to be treated based on how we treat ourselves—I only wish Vivian could have realized that her greatest value comes from always valuing herself.

Knowing who we are creates a soul comfortable in autonomy. Autonomous souls are self-affirming and resolute; they understand friendship as a pathway to further strengthen an already resilient self. Autonomous souls know that friendship should never be a vehicle for jettisoning on others our personal predicaments or private dilemmas. True friendship begins by honoring ourselves—it's only then that we can truly honor others. My hope is that Vivian will find the strength within to know she is a human treasure worthy of the utmost care. I want Vivian to one day look in the mirror and know the reflection she sees will always be worthy of love, compassion, and respect, and that no man could care for her body and soul the way that committed self-loving can.

Five

Woman Overboard

*"It would be wonderful to enjoy success without
seeing envy in the eyes of those around you."*

— *Marilyn Monroe*

I have for many years been the intermediary for women searching for themselves, and I'm grateful for the opportunity to serve them in some of their
darkest hours. As their friend, and as a friend to myself, I believe it to be
my responsibility to ensure their safety and well-being against all odds.
Committing to being a friend is like a marriage—it's for better or worse. And
for it to prosper, it must be a two-way street with free-flowing traffic, never
reaching a dead end or coming to a screeching halt.

Some years ago, I met a woman named Claire at my neighborhood grocery store. I'm a firm believer that a closed mouth doesn't get fed, so I take
every opportunity I can to network and meet new people, particularly other
women. I listened as this woman described her line of work in real estate, taking mental notes in case I or anyone I knew ever required her services.

I introduced myself, we exchanged numbers, and I contacted her shortly
thereafter to follow up. As we got to talking, it turned out she was also in need
of my hair replacement services, so we scheduled time to meet and get the ball
rolling.

We worked together for about three months before she started entrusting me with her private affairs. As I had done hundreds of times in the past, I dispensed advice and hoped she would find it useful. I was happy to see that the more we talked, the more she asked for guidance. It's moments like these that I am so proud of the woman I am, having had the fortune of choosing my independence and self-love to help women rebuild themselves from some of the lowest points of their lives. Claire was no exception—she soon took to calling me "Auntie Helen," a nickname many women have assigned me as a term of endearment. The honor of being viewed as a leader in their lives humbles me. I strive daily to remain truthful to its ideology.

Claire soon began to contact me more, asking me to her home and introducing me to her children as her mentor. I humbly accepted the honor, pleased to share a few pearls of wisdom here and there. Claire was in her early 30s, but the fact that she was close in age to my daughter made me ready and willing to do what I could to help her make her way in this world.

She was a petite Asian woman who, despite her diminutive stature, wore the pants in her family of a husband and three small rambunctious boys. Her boys were certainly a handful, but were also her "miracle children." Claire confided in me as our relationship grew that she battled daily with a painful reproductive disorder, and it was her journey into motherhood that ultimately brought her to my door. Not only was she engaged in an ongoing battle with trying to conceal the resulting bald patches in her hair—a side effect of the disease—but she also grieved over the fact that, with her diagnosis, having children would be at best challenging, and at worst, impossible.

And so it was with extra special care that I tried to help Claire always be her most beautiful, best self. Her long, jet black hair—made even more graceful with the hair prosthesis I'd designed to cover the balding patches—framed her pale-yellow skin and high cheekbones. And the dark-brown pupils that filled her beautiful moon-shaped eye sockets seemed to smile all by themselves whenever we were together. I affectionately named her "Sunshine Eyes," and was happy that she and her high-school sweetheart husband—who had been with her through all her reproductive challenges—could finally enjoy their happiest moments together doting on their children. She still fought daily to keep her disorder in check, but the love on her face that shone through whenever she mentioned her babies made all the thinning hair, weight gain, and mood swings worth the effort.

As a part-time stay-at-home mom, Claire dedicated as much time as she could to her "miracle babies," making sure she was there to meet their every need. She and her husband, a lecturer at the local community college, lived reasonably comfortably on her husband's salary. Like many families, they did what was necessary to put food on the table and be great parents to their children. And, like many families in America, they faced some of their biggest challenges ever when the Great Recession hit in 2007. For the first time in all their years together, Claire's husband's job lay in a semi-permanent state of flux, and their home suddenly lost the years of equity they'd hoped to use as a source of financial security. It took a ton of belt-tightening and even more prayer, but somehow, they managed to survive the crisis. I understood her struggles all too well, and I could easily empathize with the difficulties she was facing. I was proud of Claire and her husband's determination to survive the economic downturn and even prouder of their commitment to keep their family together under such duress.

The Fearless Leap Faithfully into Niagara Falls

Claire and her husband's proven commitment to being successful family providers made me want to refer Claire to potential customers and anyone in our respective networks as often as I could. Our biggest opportunity came about eight months into our relationship, when I received a work invitation from a very public figure. I typically handle these kinds of assignments myself, but this one required an insurmountable amount of work. And having worked with Claire, I knew she had the skills to handle a key portion of this project.

For years I've worked in the private environments of public figures—whether I'm in the mansions of moguls, the abodes of billionaires, or the sanctuaries of celebrities, enhancing and reconstructing the crowning glory of a famous woman is for me simply another day at the office. My personal rule dictates that, given the intimacy of information disclosed to me as their designated healer, my clients both public and private are entitled to complete confidentiality—selfies, gossip, and the insatiable need for distributing private confidences on social media is forbidden. I have a host of secrets revealed to me by famous faces that will forever stay locked in our shared scared space— loyalty to the individual behind a famous face has no price, yet it's the thing riches cannot buy.

For Claire, on the other hand, I knew the chance to hob-nob with some famous faces would be a plus to the hours-long obligations needed to complete our task. Provided she abide by my privacy rules, she was welcome aboard—in a few short weeks we would be enjoying the celebrity faces at a golf tournament in Lake Tahoe, California, interspersing our hard work with a few hours of rest and relaxation at the 17th hole. A part of me celebrated inwardly—I had a friend and associate I could count on who could commit to getting the work done without coming undone in in the presence of celebrity and wealth.

So it was with great surprise and frustration that I witnessed Claire's reaction at the end of one of our work days on site. While she was unassuming at work with our public client, she was wild and unrestrained at the event after-party. Unbeknownst to me, Claire was a huge fan of five-time MVP and two-time NBA Hall of Fame inductee Michael Jordan, who was attending the golf tournament that year. I hadn't noticed his entrance until Claire grabbed my arm, half-yanking me to the floor, shouting "He's a god" at the top of her lungs. I tried to restrain her and remind her that as colleagues of our client, we were expected to rise above such childish behavior. Inwardly, I was both surprised and somewhat angry—I was sure Claire's self-confidence was so strong that she considered no one more important than herself.

I somehow managed to get Claire to collect herself, grabbing a chair and virtually ordering her to get herself together. I was here on business, and I wasn't about to let Claire's crazy-celebrity-infatuation negatively affect my image. About an hour later, Mr. Jordan approached our table and took a seat next to me. We shook hands and smiled at one another, indicating our mutual respect. To the outside world he was arguably one of the greatest athletes of all time, but what I understood Mr. Jordan to be during the several hours I spent getting to know him was a person who appreciated the wisdom and personal power of two hard-working people. We talked and laughed about many things, but most importantly celebrated our mutual determination to rise above others' expectations. We may have been two of only a handful of African Americans in the room, but we were proud to stand in our own versions of success.

"His Airness" was at one point so comfortable he took a seat in my lap and hugged me around my waist, the way a brother and sister might celebrate one another's company. Together we celebrated the community of two people who understood that a body surrounded by riches is only enriched with the presence of priceless souls. Claire watched in awe, secretly revealing to me later that if she were me, she would "never wash those pants again." Poor Claire was still missing the point—autonomous women need not reduce anyone to a mere object of desire; they will instead welcome an individual into their world in the hopes each of them can better one another.

If I couldn't count on Claire to remain composed at a celebrity event, I could always count on my best friend and business partner Allison to back me up. Mr. Jordan was accompanied at that time by his then girlfriend Yvette Prieto, who would later become his wife and the mother of their two children. As a woman who always puts my sisters first, my instinct was to ensure Yvette was comfortable with the goings on at our table, knowing that she may have felt like a bit of an outsider with all the attention focused on her fiancé. Sensing my desire for inclusion, Allison rushed to my aid—she put her arm around Yvette's shoulders as she introduced herself and pulled Yvette in for a hug. Allison had already done the math in her head. Yvette was a non-Black woman and a former model; she was also what some considered "the other woman" in Mr. Jordan's life—she appeared in the public eye after the very publicized divorce of Mr. Jordan from his first wife of 17 years. Allison could almost hear the voices in the heads of the women around her aimed at Yvette, as their eye rolls and frowns indicated their envy—and some disgust—of Yvette's position.

Allison put a stop to that immediately, letting Yvette know she was welcome to spend as much time with our team of women as she liked. I think Mr. Jordan was also impressed with Allison's behavior—he grabbed the arm of Allison closest to him that was hugging his fiancé and kissed the back of

Allison's hand as if to say, "thank you for showing my woman some love." It was our pleasure to bring just a bit of happiness to this happy couple whose private affairs had placed them in a public struggle with the weight of celebrity. I've often said one doesn't have to be a billionaire to have a billionaire's mind, but a billion pounds of self-esteem opens doors to a prosperous future. Allison and I hoped we'd proven to Claire that rising above the expectations of others is a direct result of women being firmly planted in themselves. When we make ourselves our primary investment, we achieve our best riches, and I was happy our team could make Mr. Jordan and Ms. Prieto's night just a bit richer.

Caught in a Rip Current

I was hopeful after our last project together that Claire would start to gain a better appreciation for her skills and what she'd achieved. She'd been in a room full of people with varying degrees of wealth and fame, and I'd hoped that what it taught her was at any given time she could have more than some and less than others, but she should never allow her economic position to dictate her personal version of success. The path to happiness starts with full embrace of the life she has.

But instead, I think our work together was having the opposite effect. A few months into the early part of our relationship Claire and I worked together on a media project that would be mutually beneficial to our businesses. When the day came for us both to disclose a portion of our financials as a requisite for participation, I had zero concerns about Claire getting wind of my information—I believed that as a business woman her focus would be solely on creating a rewarding event. We happily endured long days and sleepless nights until the campaign came to a satisfying end, and continued to celebrate our partnership for months to come. I felt nothing for our past work experience but joy and excitement for our next opportunities.

About a week after the completion of our celebrity event, as I was putting the final touches on an intricate design of a client's prosthetic, a call came in from Claire. I make it a point to interrupt work only if necessary, and since

Claire was a business colleague I anticipated delivery of important news. A part of me was still celebrating the previous week's success—I smiled to myself as I read her name on caller ID and eagerly picked up her call.

But as I hung up the phone about 30 minutes later, a sense of frustration overwhelmed me. I tried to talk myself out of the negative feelings I was experiencing, but to no avail—I was angry, and had to do my best to keep from letting my emotions ruin my day. I didn't want the dinner plans I'd scheduled with Allison spoiled by Claire's behavior. I took a deep breath, determined not to let Claire's last comments frustrate me.

As I greeted Allison that evening at the door of our favorite sushi restaurant, I tried hard to have my frustrations in check. But I knew better than to keep a secret from my closest friend and confidant—Allison is the "Real Deal Holyfield" of friends and the fact that we are so much alike means she can see past my smile on any day. Her emotional quotient rivals mine, her integrity is off the charts, and she's willing to take on anybody or anything that could be a problem for me. I knew if I didn't do my best to take the frown off my face, Claire would later surely have it coming from Allison.

Allison also has an entirely different model of what a human being should be, and that makes her very demanding when it comes to developing friendships—in her mind, most people just don't measure up. She once told me that "most people can't be the kind of friend to me that I need." That's when I knew Allison was the one for me. I took a deep breath and admitted to myself I wasn't going to be able to protect Claire this time. Before Allison could ask what was wrong, I blurted it out.

"I wish Claire would stop trying to count my money."

Allison knew immediately what I meant. She'd had experience with this before—she looked me straight in the eye and waited for me to tell her how this seemingly perfect friendship had come down to this. Unfortunately, I had to admit my greatest fear had been realized—inviting Claire to work with my prosperous clientele had sealed the deal— I was now, in her eyes, "one of them," instead of "us." During the months we'd worked together I'd often hear Claire complain about the "greed" of an associate who cleared a-million-plus yearly in commissions, but when I'd make suggestions about what she could do to reach that career goal, she'd scoff at the work required and make excuses for why she couldn't do it. I realized in her phone call that the combination of seeing my financials and being a part of my work environment reminded her of what she hadn't accomplished—I was now no better than the "million-dollar-snobs" who out-commissioned her daily. I tried hard not to shed even the slightest tear in front of Allison—in my mind Claire and I were a team regardless of our income and career stature, but to Claire this was a line of separation that couldn't be crossed.

I reluctantly admitted to Allison that within a few months after she'd given me the title of "Auntie Helen," Claire casually started alluding to her financial challenges in our conversations. Before long, she'd taken to asking me for short-term loans on anything from a few hundred to thousands of dollars. In the beginning, I think since she'd elevated me to a "mentor," she believed it was okay for her to ingratiate herself to me financially. In retrospect, I realized that Claire in a small way resented what she found as she learned more about my business. I was heartbroken over the realization that what began as an alliance of two powerful women was morphing into an unhealthy friendship based solely on money.

I started telling Allison about all the financial help I'd given Claire and all the promises she'd made to get it back to me. I'd helped with bills that were overdue and projects for her children that needed additional funding. At first I thought I was just helping out a friend, but the more I helped, the more I was asked to contribute. "I just have to get this one thing straightened out first," Claire would say to me, then I could expect a quick turnaround on my loan. And on the occasions that I did try to let her know I just didn't have it this time, she would shoot me a calculating look to remind me that she had intimate knowledge of my personal finances and would be the final authority on what I could loan. Claire would then proceed to remind me of all the things she'd done for me "for free." She'd run through the list of how she'd aided me, as though I was a kind of line item in her accounting spreadsheet. She'd draw constant comparisons between my income and hers, and scathingly assume that since I was self-employed I had on-demand access to infinite funds. Never mind that she and her family were living better than most people they knew—even with all their previous challenges, they'd managed to create a pretty sizeable nest egg and were living quite comfortably.

I also shared with Allison that I secretly took note of the amount of money Claire spent on non-essential items. As she'd lament about her mortgage, utilities, and general cost of living, I couldn't help but notice the receipts for expensive family vacations and high-end luxury purses and shoes that sometimes spilled from her wallet. Allison once referred to Claire's habit as the "buy what you want, then beg for what you need" syndrome, and the scowl forming on her face made it clear she disapproved of Claire's behavior. I could see Allison plotting about what she would say to Claire as soon as she had the opportunity.

This wasn't the first time Allison and Claire had discussed finances. When Allison noticed Claire and I were developing a working relationship, she quietly pulled her aside and gave her a stern warning in private.

"I really like you Claire," she said. "I think you're great at what you do, and it's so refreshing to have you on the team. But I want to make something very clear."

"I know you and Helen have exchanged money for each other's services, and I also know she's helped you out a bit here and there. Helen is a kind and generous woman; we both know that if she had 10 cents, she'd give up nine just to make sure she wouldn't have to watch someone suffer. I know she loves you and you love her. But please don't take this money thing too far—Helen has a business to run and a family to feed, so as long as that's respected, everything will be fine." Apparently, Claire hadn't gotten the message—but I knew this time Allison was going to make sure it came through loud and clear.

Allison gave me some time to vent, then excused herself from the table and stepped outside. I knew she was hurt that yet another woman had come into my life with the same pretense: She is anxious to be friends, but eventually her interaction with me becomes more about what I can give her than how we can support one another. Claire was about to get a tongue-lashing that even I couldn't give. I sat with my head down, but I could hear Allison's muffled voice starting to raise. At first, she was definitive and direct, then erratic, and soon after, completely uncontrolled. This went on for about 15 minutes straight. Nope, Allison was not about to go easy on Claire. I thought about trying to intervene because I knew Claire's back was against the wall. I had unloaded onto Allison everything Claire said to me and told her what I felt like Claire was saying behind my back when she couldn't get me to pay her bills. But most important, I told Allison that Claire must have asked me a hundred times to "keep this between us"—Claire wanted neither her husband nor Allison to know that I was loaning her money. I knew for that reason alone Allison was going to get all up in Claire's business, and read her from left to right.

Lesson Three: Don't Let a Monsoon Trouble a Smooth-Running River

After Allison had verbally "knocked Claire into next week," I decided never again to lend Claire money. I've lamented for years that women who aren't on a path to emotional, economic, mental, or spiritual oneness remain on a frantic search for gaining the fundamental understanding of who they are. Until they characterize and define their own sense of unique identity, they take every opportunity to gorge on the fortitude of strong people. Sure, it makes sense to nourish ourselves on the strengths of those around us, particularly our friends and family, but feasting on the energy of others to avoid addressing our own shortcomings is another matter.

As strong of a woman as I believed Claire to be, her weakness was not being able to embrace her own unique power. Instead, she sought out anything—people, material things, money—that she believed could bring her power. Whether it was coveting another's success, or using relationships solely as a reservoir to drain financial and/or emotional reserves, Claire made others responsible for filling the gaps created by her lack of ability to believe in herself.

Claire's own achievements were never enough—the more time we spent together, the more our conversations hinged upon money. Between hints about how nice it would be to have a fancy car and a bigger house, and saccharin-laced comments about my "jet-set life with celebrities," I was overwhelmed. Anything Claire said was met with a scowl she tried unsuccessfully to hide through a smile—I soon became her excuse to downplay her accomplishments and second-guess her life choices. All the things that were important to her—raising her children, managing her real estate career, and contributing to the life she and her husband built—now took a back seat to my finances and career achievements whenever we were together.

What I also discovered about Claire was that she was unwilling to use the success of others as motivation to work harder and realize her greatest potential—she preferred instead either to ride the coattails of those who'd realized theirs or envy their incredible drive to succeed.

As motivated as Claire was to work with me, she was equally unmotivated to build up her career—any suggestion of continuing her education, taking on work that increased publicity but didn't pay, or adding more hours to her plate to help her reach her goals—was met with irritation and impatience. Her complaints about not earning enough were never-ending—it seemed everything and everyone around Claire fueled her ongoing dissatisfaction with her life.

I could only hope that one day Claire would lose her voracious appetite for comparing herself with others and learn to find contentment in her life. I spent my formative years in the public housing community of one of the wealthiest cities in the world, yet never begrudged the success of those around me. My expectations for a successful life were so high that no amount of wealth or celebrity could intimidate me or make me feel inadequate, even when I didn't have a penny to my name. As a little girl I considered myself a "rich-minded" thinker, and that line of thinking set in motion a series of events I believed were necessary to bring my goals to fruition.

Lesson Four: A Celebrity Lifestyle Requires a Celebrity Mind

My years of interacting with wealthy people taught me that, among other things, levels of financial success are often proportional to the amount of risk and hard work invested—it makes no sense to want a vacation home and a Rolls Royce but not be willing to undergo the extreme sacrifices needed to get them. I also learned that no matter how much work we put into getting the life we want, sometimes things just don't turn out the way we planned. As a business owner, I've had plenty of failures—some might say more than my fair share. But I've accepted my achievements and failures equally. What I always keep top of mind is that my life is exactly where it's supposed to be. Using all my energy to throw shade into the limelight of others won't make my life any easier, and certainly won't help me be better. I choose instead to embrace my life as it is and define for myself who and what I wish to be.

What saddens me about Claire is that her "poor mind" continues to convince her she is entitled to sail on a ship filled with silver and gold, yet the only sacrifices she's willing to make are those that procure iron and ore. Claire fails to understand that if her sense of self was pure and strong, she would not define herself through material things, no matter how much or how little she had—she would instead be an impenetrable fortress of self-esteem, daring others to be a part of her world instead of begging to be a part of everyone else's.

I've always said that money and possessions are okay to have if we know how to have them—I've asked people numerous times if they would still want to drive a fancy car if no one was around to watch them drive it. If the answer is Yes, then I know they are focused on achieving their personal best. But if the answer is No, then it's clear to me the focus is on gaining material things solely to feel some sense of one-upmanship, or to disempower others who are building their own dreams. I think Claire struggles daily with this kind of scenario. Her inability to fully recognize her own power means she will forever be second-guessing her abilities and letting others define her place in this world. My hope is that Claire can take some time for personal reflection and realize her prosperity lies in letting go of her obsession with worshipping the almighty dollar. If she learns to understand that anything gained in life should be to only satisfy her personal best, then she will consider anything she does to be a great success.

It's the opposite of this kind of thinking that keeps "poor-minded" Claire from being all she can be. She has the intelligence to be at the top of her game but lacks the belief in herself and the drive needed to get there. Her Achille's heel is wanting others to hand to her the version of success to which she believes she's entitled, yet she resents those who have the audacity to occupy a space of greatness she believes belongs only to her. This is a sad concept for me to grasp since I've always believed my personal power is priceless—whether I had something or nothing, my resolve to achieve my personal best never waned. I have vivid memories of fighting off hundreds of rats and roaches from Aaron's and Isabel's cribs as I struggled to keep the rent paid in our tiny run-down apartment—even then, I knew I belonged amongst leaders, great thinkers, and pillars of the community. It is not from where you come that defines you; it's knowing where you are going.

Six

CHALLENGER DEEP

"I will prove by my life that my critics are liars."

— *PLATO*

Given my commitment to women's well-being, I often wonder what would have become of the women I know had I met them earlier in life—time had so broken some of my sisters that only a vestige of a fully-calibrated She-Compass remained by the time we came together. My best friend Allison fit this description. Here was a woman devoted to being a supporter of women everywhere, but she struggled greatly to forge her own identity.

Allison and I met by accident—she was working full time for an advertising agency in the Bay Area and I was in the early stages of building my dream salon. By chance, I drove into the parking lot of a coffee shop I'd never been to before as I made my way to an offsite concierge appointment. Allison had just ordered her daily latte and was rushing out the door as I was coming in. She stopped me, looked at my hair, and told me it was one of the best haircuts and color blends she'd ever seen.

I was intrigued by the woman staring back at me—I smiled as she complimented my hair, outfit, and overall personality. I watched her light brown eyes, initially focused on grabbing her keys and getting quickly to her car, widen with excitement as she looked at me and spoke. This tall, statuesque, imposing woman—wearing a black knee-length pencil skirt, a pair of black pump kitten heels and a robust red blazer over a flattering soft white silk blouse—was clearly poised to take on the corporate world. She appeared to be in her early 20s, but I sensed her maturity level was well beyond her chronological age. As we enjoyed a firm handshake, wisps of her Jacklyn-Smith-inspired, slightly wavy, shoulder-length hair softly kissed her smooth slightly tanned White skin.

I smiled at her broadly, embracing her words on behalf of my fellow hair loss sisters—it felt good to see this beautiful woman with a very full mane of her own hair take such interest in a hairpiece. When I leaned in and whispered to her that I was a balding woman wearing a prosthetic, her mouth dropped open, and she immediately asked for my number. She said she had two associates who could use my services; I thanked her and we went our separate ways.

About a month later she contacted me and soon after came to see me with her referrals. We all chatted for a while—my new clients shared with me everything from their medical histories, to their favorite movies, to their views about the world. We had a pleasant visit and discussed next steps for their hair health. At the end of their consultation, I escorted my three beautiful ladies to the door and said my goodbyes until our next appointment.

About 15 minutes later, Allison returned to the door and said she wanted to talk to me about my business. She asked what kind of marketing plan I had in place. I explained that since much of my work came by referral, aggressive marketing wasn't very high on the priority list. This was also long before social media made it acceptable to publicly discuss—or even mention—hair replacement for women.

Allison explained that she really believed in what I was doing, and if I would allow it, she would like to find a way to appropriately publicize my story—free of charge—with as many people that would listen. On top of the fact that I wasn't comfortable "outing" balding women, I'd also never been offered anything without some kind of price, so needless to say I was skeptical in the beginning. But Allison slowly brought me on board, carefully crafting a story that was met with public acceptance and didn't compromise the respect due to special-needs clients. We worked together a project at a time until Allison had a full marketing program in place. All this while she was still working for her agency, and never once did she ask for any form of compensation. This was proof in my belief of the power of sisterhood—once these bonds are in place they are hard to break.

Allison continued helping me with my business, and before long grew to be the person on whom I could depend to keep things moving. We regularly planned and executed a host of marketing and sales ideas, and met for lunches, movies, and nights out as often as we could. Though I was a few years older, we were both still enjoying our 20s and happily spent hours talking about the great futures we'd planned. I celebrated that, for once, I had met a woman whose version of friendship was the same as mine.

But what I also came to realize was that as committed as Allison was to being a great friend, she was just as unsure about her own sense of self. Outwardly, Allison appeared to have it all—a great career, solid plans for her future, and a no-nonsense approach to living her life. But inwardly Allison was a woman who needed help breaking open the locked box that concealed her true self-worth—I soon learned I had Allison's upbringing to thank for this.

Like me, Allison was raised in a single-parent household. Her father died before she was born, so she was the only one of her three older siblings who had no memory of him. She told me her childhood was filled with a strange sense of emptiness—her mother, siblings, aunts, and uncles gushed about how much her father loved his family, but Allison felt robbed of the opportunity to enjoy his love.

She tried hard to envision the closeness to her father her family had, especially when her brother or sisters would talk about his laid back, level-headed personality. He was comfortable around all types of people, and those who knew him appreciated his ability to immediately put people at ease. He was also intensely focused and matter-of-fact when it came to providing for his family. A landscaper by trade, he especially appreciated people who worked hard but were challenged to make ends meet; he understood all too well the difficultly in living paycheck to paycheck and was fiercely determined that one day he would provide his wife and children a comfortable future.

Allison told me one of the things her aunts loved most about him was how he would use his "way with words" to get things done. A man who'd barely graduated high school, his conversational skills seemed to run circles around those of a Rhodes scholar. I laughed alongside Allison when she shared a story her Aunt had relayed about her father using his "power of conversation" to secure a small stake in an exclusive financial transaction open only to members of a prestigious private social group. Allison's father always had his nose to the grind and paid close attention anytime his boss—a wealthy homeowner of a vast estate—talked shop. This time it was a phone call the homeowner took by the pool that piqued Allison's father's interest—he was all ears and took copious mental notes.

To the owner of the four-acre property where her father worked, Allison's father's only purpose was to keep the lawn well mowed and the foliage properly pruned—the homeowner made it a point not to interact with "the help" unless it was absolutely necessary.

But Allison's father was a big thinker, and when it came to caring for his family, an even bigger dreamer. Allison's father processed everything he heard the homeowner discuss—before long he had a host of business ideas lined up.

So when the homeowner approached Allison's father one day with a huge complaint about a section of the garden, Allison's father saw his opportunity. Adept at playing the "I'm just a laborer, what do I know?" role, he nodded his head, apologized for the error and promised to fix the problem. It's when Allison's father casually congratulated the homeowner on how well his investments were paying off that the homeowner took note, surprised that a laborer would have the slightest idea about managing investments. Turns out the "gardener" knew more than for what the homeowner gave him credit—not only did Allison's father convince the homeowner to let him in on the exclusive deal, Allison's father showed the homeowner how to significantly increase his profit margin. The homeowner never looked at "the help" the same way again.

Allison said stories like these gave her a strong appreciation for the man her father was, but what was missing was the opportunity to experience the love he had for her. I had the fortune of carrying with me into adulthood the love my Dad had for me, even if I'd only had him in my life for a short time. I couldn't imagine trying to create that feeling based solely on the descriptions of others. To make matters worse, I learned that Allison's sense of loss was made greater by the presence of the one parent she had left.

Allison's mother was the complete opposite of her father—while her father was practical and non-confrontational, her mother was ill-tempered, manic, and vengeful. While her father wanted nothing more than to provide for and protect his children, her mother lived to rule over the offspring. She relished the creation and enforcement of unrealistic household rules—at the very top of the list was the forbiddance of any level of self-awareness or self-expression. Opinions, points of view, and all forms of communication not coupled with downcast eyes and shrunken shoulders were considered disrespectful, and this "having an attitude" behavior was cause for severe punishment.

Allison's mother controlled everything from what her children said to what they thought. Constantly reminding her charges that "I will always know you better than you know yourself," she made sure she was the final authority on the very state of their being.

It was because of this dichotomy to which Allison was exposed—knowing she was loved by one parent she'd never known, but not knowing what love felt like from the other who'd raised her since birth—that her She-Compass needed complete recalibration. She was so broken that it took a mishap to expose her deepest wounds.

Navigational Hazard Ahead

About a year into my friendship with Allison, I invited her to a family get together. Given my mother's relationship with Ralph, I'd seen more than my fair share of family chaos. Although I preferred the quiet sounds of classical music and the calmness of low-toned voices, I understood that for some members of my family, yelling over a booming stereo or screaming our conversations across a room was the only version of an inside voice many of us knew. We'd holler out nonsensical answers to non-existent questions and took every opportunity to talk louder than the last person talking. And as our mother would line the table with food, then announce which members of the family she had assigned to this year's lineup of "the talent show," the ruckus would only get worse. For hours I'd find a way to sit through the noise, but the love I felt for my family made it all worthwhile.

For Allison, our family event was a completely different experience. After about an hour of listening to my siblings and I scream and holler at each other about one casual subject after another, Allison had had enough. As politely as she could, she excused herself from the room, made a comment about needing to briefly get some air, and calmly walked outside. Allison was the picture of perfection when it came to manners and respect, but inside she was a ball of nerves. I didn't realize she was troubled until I noticed that another hour had passed and she hadn't come back inside.

I went outside to check on her—and saw her sitting in the driver's seat of her car, her sweaty palms wiping tears from her face. I immediately asked her what was wrong as I climbed into the passenger seat next to her. She tried as best she could to tell me about the range of emotions flooding her body—though she was okay with the obvious affection my family had for one another, the cacophony of voices we used to express that love completely unnerved her. She'd never witnessed chaos in a family that wasn't a prelude to something much worse. For Allison, screaming and yelling were an overture to acts of verbal and physical attack.

I listened as Allison sobbed, knowing it must have taken an incredibly strong will for this emotionally guarded woman to break down. Unlike the women who'd come into my life before her, Allison wasn't looking for someone to save her. She was the one who saved others. Allison knew how to be a solid rock, and she used that strength to build up other women. I realized the best way to help was simply to lend an attentive ear—I knew the woman who'd spent so much of her life solving the dilemmas of others finally needed someone to help solve hers.

Vertigo

Despite being clearly upset, Allison tried hard to remain composed. In between sobs, she'd angrily wipe away tears and stare straight ahead in silence. She apologized profusely for "letting my emotions get the best of me," and repeatedly told me she didn't want to be viewed as "some helpless creature" needing rescue. When I told her it was completely okay to cry if she was in pain, she shot me a look of irritation. I'd never met someone so frustrated with showing emotion, but I knew if I waited patiently Allison would eventually share with me the hurt that lived deep inside her.

I searched her face for information, but the stone look on her face told me she would express herself only when she was ready. I took that opportunity to go back inside the house and let my family know I'd be leaving. I convinced Allison to let me drive her home, then sat with her in her living room for another hour while she stared blankly at TV and flipped her remote nonchalantly through its channels. Then completely unexpectedly, she spoke.

She told me her earliest memories of emotional and physical abuse started in kindergarten. The scenario was always the same—happy moments quickly became nightmares.

In one memory, Allison's "happy moment" began when she arrived at her front door, fresh from a kindergarten day filled with paper bag puppets and show-and-tell. The lemony-smell of freshly polished furniture, coupled with the rich, full-bodied alto voices of Karen Carpenter and Gladys Knight emanating from the living room stereo enveloped her in a sense of warmth. The lines in the just-vacuumed, thick navy-blue carpet made her want to kick off her shoes and press her toes firmly into the plush fabric. For one brief moment, Allison dreamt of being like other kids, wishing her mother would appear with a plate of freshly baked cookies and a hug—she fantasized about the two of them sitting in the seat of the large family room bay window, laughing about the events of Allison's school day.

With her mother-daughter fantasy fresh in her mind, Allison smiled to herself and skipped through the hallway to her mother's room, hoping to greet her with a hug and kiss the moment she laid eyes on her. She could picture her mother's face and imagine the slight fragrance of her perfume—Allison couldn't wait to press her face against the apron that always laid perfectly on her mother's waistline.

The little dream she'd crafted was usually met with cold reality. Allison would soon find her mother crouched down on the right side of her bed in her housecoat, a towel swathed around her freshly washed hair, crying uncontrollably. Allison would stop in her tracks when she'd see her mother in this familiar position, a position that would become so commonplace that Allison began drawing up mental plans for how to sacrifice her own life in exchange for her mother's well-being.

Seasick

By the time Allison reached first grade, she'd had what seemed like a lifetime of practice facing her mother's inexplicable crying fits. Allison believed for a while that if she was just "nicer" to her mother, she could take away whatever turmoil she was experiencing. But Allison's concern frequently turned to confusion and pain when her mother's crying turned to alarming rage about the smallest details. Ultimately, Allison learned to hold back tears—or any emotion—and instead focus on apologizing profusely simply for being born.

Allison shared with me one story about the first day of school. Allison was excited to be walking finally in the footsteps of her three older siblings—done with kindergarten, she was now attending grade school "like the big kids." She was looking forward to making friends, but her biggest excitement of the day was getting to ride the school bus for the first time.

Grinning at the opportunity to finally wear her brand-new school clothes—a short sleeved sky-blue-and-white checkered-patterned dress with a clock pendant attached to its ruffled collar—Allison hopped into the family station wagon, admiring her matching navy-blue tights and dark blue buckle shoes while she sat quietly as her mother drove to the bus stop. She smiled to herself, knowing this was the beginning of a great day.

Her mother waited in the car with Allison as the bus arrival time inched closer. Once the clock said two minutes to 8:00 am, Allison climbed out of the station wagon and made her way a few feet over to the spot where the bus would pick her up. She waited anxiously about a minute more— finally the bus pulled up and Allison climbed onto the bottom step. That's when she immediately heard a car horn blaring in the background. She turned around to see her mother laying defiantly on the horn of the family car, wildly waving her hands through the windshield at Allison.

Completely dumbfounded, Allison looked at the bus driver and then back at her mother. She knew this was the bus that would take her to school, but her mother's unrelenting horn honking disoriented and confused Allison. She froze. The bus driver, by now impatient and ready to get going, asked if she was boarding. Allison looked back at her mother, then at him, paralyzed by fear and unsure how to answer.

Now clearly irritated, the bus driver ordered Allison off the bus. Humiliated by her mother's erratic behavior, Allison felt the other kids staring at her as she stepped down. She wished there were a hundred stairs at that moment—all she wanted was to descend as far away possible from this hurtful and embarrassing situation.

As she slowly made her way back to the car, Allison braced herself for her mother's oncoming wrath—she knew the punishment for not getting on the bus was going to be severe. Sure enough, the moment Allison climbed into the station wagon, Allison's mother fired off a host of expletives and accusations. Allison endured the yelling and screaming, trying to explain to her mother that the frenetic honking confused her—she was sure her mother's behavior indicated Allison wasn't to board the bus at all. It was at that moment Allison watched her mother's Jekyll-and-Hyde transformation—without warning, Allison's mother leaned in, grabbed the collar of Allison's dress, pulled Allison to her face and shook her wildly. "You're a liar! You missed the damn bus just so I would drive you to school, you ungrateful little troublemaker! You're always trying to get attention—I'm so damn sick and tired of you lying to me!" As Allison's head reeled and wobbled from the force of her mother's shaking, she felt the back of her mother's hand swipe across her face. Allison was hit with such force, the blow left a deep red indention on her cheek. She did her best not to shed tears, lest another wallop land on her other cheek. Allison clutched her dress and tried to focus—she learned from that point on that pain was best managed by being shut down, and that feelings were best managed by being shut off.

Iceberg Ahead

In between silent sobs and a trembling jaw that could barely get the words out, Allison told me that each time her mother assaulted her verbally or physically it felt like she'd been run over by an 18-wheeler big rig. The pupils in her mother's dark brown eyes, when angry, would become so dilated that she appeared almost demonic. It took everything I had not shed tears with her, as I could only imagine what it must have been like for a small child to have to endure this kind of daily abuse from a person she believed she could trust.

I knew reliving these terrible memories must have been devastating for Allison—of the 4 children in her family, she was the child who most longed to bring joy to others, so to have that innate kindness beaten out of her daily must have made her wonder if she was no more than an empty shell. Allison told me that to avoid seeing her mother she would retreat to her backyard for hours to play in the grass and pick flowers after school—she'd do her best to arrange the carnations, azaleas, and calla lilies she'd picked into a bouquet, then deliver them to the homes of everyone in her neighborhood. She told me she did it to "make the grown-ups smile." And during outings with her mother, she remembered wanting to hug everyone that passed her by. Her mother forbade any kind of affection with strangers, so Allison settled for looking right into each passerby's eyes and smiling. The smiles she received in return were the proof she needed to believe that not all adults were bad people.

I sat with Allison for a few more hours that night, then as we said our goodbyes, I made her promise that we would continue this talk. I wanted Allison to know our getting together to heal was not just a one-off, and that no matter how long it took, I would be there for her. From that moment on, we agreed to chat on the phone or meet up as often as we could.

One Sunday we met at Golden Gate Park for a picnic. We started our talk the usual way, chatting about small details before we eased into specifics of her painful childhood. I could see by the look in her eyes—first wistfulness and contentment, then sadness, then devastation—that Allison was working extra hard to revive memories she'd suppressed years ago. So when she took a deep breath and proceeded to tell me about one particularly painful memory, I reached out and tightly held her hand. I braced myself for the oncoming wave, prepared to swim by Allison's side as long as she needed me to.

Boiler Room

By the time Allison was 13, she had plans to flee her mother's house. Even if the pain her mother inflicted gave her little in life to look forward to, she knew she'd have zero chance at a life of any kind if she didn't get away soon.

Allison's mother was laser-focused on owning her daughter's body and soul, so Allison began enacting Operation Getaway as quickly as she could. Her key act of resistance was to hyper focus on school, aiming all her attention on outdoing her classmates in GPA, extra-curricular activities, and in landing the academic scholarship that would carry her away from this hell. She would prove by her accomplishments that everything her mother said about her was a lie.

When I asked Allison how the rest of her family fared against her mother's behavior, she paused and looked quietly into the distance. When she spoke again she told me that at one time she'd hoped her older brother and sisters would protect her from their mother's volatile behavior, but her siblings learned early in life that defying their mother was futile and could only further threaten their safety. While he was alive, Allison's father made it clear to her siblings that raising children was "women's work," and he had no plans to intervene in his wife's running of the household. Her siblings learned early on to keep quiet and let the chips fall where they may. By the time Allison was born, her siblings had become so brainwashed by the abuse they'd endured that it was easier to let their naïve younger sister fend for herself than to stand up to the matriarch who bullied the household. Allison would later surmise that even if her father had been unwilling to admit his wife was mentally ill, she and her siblings might have had a completely different childhood had her father been more willing to be involved in his children's care at home.

Allison shared with me that once, when her mother was away, Allison was beaten for speaking up during a playdate with her siblings. The matter was simple. Allison didn't want to play a family game of four square with a ball that belonged to her brother—it was slightly deflated and wouldn't bounce properly. To Allison, the solution was easy: She'd made so many friends from her flower delivery days that she had no trouble at all getting a loaner ball from the little girl next door. In 10 minutes, Allison had procured a brand-new ball that was so well inflated it could bounce sky-high.

Her siblings, however, saw two things very wrong with this situation. First, Allison had the audacity to want a ball that didn't belong to her—complaining about anything, even if there was something obviously wrong with it, was considered defiant, and her older siblings couldn't wait to tell their mother that Allison was "talking back and being flippant" over an issue they believed she had no right to challenge. Second, Allison left her house while her mother wasn't home. It didn't matter that she'd done no more than cross her front lawn less than 50 feet to ring the doorbell of the neighbor her family knew very well. What mattered more was that she disobeyed a rule, and the siblings smiled to themselves as they planned their revenge—they weren't about to let Allison enjoy any right to free thought or speech if they couldn't indulge in this behavior, too. By the time news of Allison's "neighborhood visit" reached her mother's ears, it had been laced with a host of falsehoods and allegations.

Each time her siblings saw Allison engage in any attempts at problem solving, speaking up, being unafraid to take a risk, or simply having the courage to live normally without fear of reprisal, it infuriated them, particularly if Allison's behavior was well within the realm of common sense. And every time her siblings reported Allison to their mother, Allison's mother relished the opportunity to make an example of Allison—she was her mother's best ammunition for keeping all her charges in line. So, with Allison as the scapegoat, everyone benefitted—the siblings could continue to concoct stories about Allison for their own gain, and Allison's mother could continue her abusive tirade against Allison, her "bad seed." Soon it became easier just to point the finger at Allison, regardless of the absurdity of the accusations leveled against her. Allison was the chosen fall guy, guilty until proven innocent. Allison told me these kinds of family attacks were common and she didn't know what hurt worse—being offered up by her siblings for punishment like Judas did Jesus, or being beaten simply for using the brains and voice God gave her.

Allison continued working on Operation Getaway until she noticed one day she could no longer see the blackboards in her classrooms. Allison learned early not to ask for help from anyone, lest she be reminded that "I've got three other kids—what makes you think you're so special?" Instead of complaining, she made whatever allowances she could—she sat as close to the front of her classrooms as possible, sometimes even asking her teachers if she could sit at their desks to get a better view. Her teachers found this admirable—they respected what they assumed was Allison's pure dedication to learning. But when one of Allison's teachers casually mentioned to Allison's mother in a parent-teacher phone call that Allison was having trouble seeing the blackboard, Allison knew she was about to be burned yet again by her mother's volcanic behavior.

Allison's mother made her annoyance at Allison clear—as she had countless times before, her mother deemed Allison's teacher's interest in Allison a result of Allison vying for unnecessary attention. Never mind that attention was the last thing Allison wanted from anyone, especially her mother.

Reluctantly, Allison's mother took her to an eye doctor on the advice of Allison's teacher, determined to prove that Allison was once again lying. Allison sat patiently through three different eye exams and the results were the same—without a doubt, Allison was going to need glasses.

Allison's better judgment always warned her to keep silent in her mother's presence, but for a brief moment, she put aside all the accusations, all the verbal and physical attacks, all the berating and browbeating she'd endured for years, in the hopes that surely her mother could see the logic in this situation. After all, the doctor had categorically confirmed Allison's vision required glasses to help her see properly—she was sure her mother understood there was no possible way Allison would lie about this.

Confident in this situation's obvious clarity, Allison took her mother's hand softly in hers and slowly let her head come to rest on her mother's shoulder. She was hoping, if only for a moment, they could be like a real mother and daughter, casually discussing the situation and talking about what kind of glasses would best suit Allison.

Allison looked up at her mother, remembering for a hopeful moment the warm feelings that would envelop her when coming home from kindergarten. In a soft voice, she spoke to her mother: "Did I do okay, Mom? I really tried to read the letters correctly in all those tests but I think I probably got most of them wrong." Allison anxiously held onto a small glimmer of hope that her mother might agree with her, just this once.

Allison's mother answered her daughter in a soft, deep monotone that began as slightly impatient and soon began reeking with annoyance. She looked straight ahead, avoiding looking in her daughter's eyes. "You want to know what I think?" Allison's mother shrugged Allison's head off her shoulder.

"I think you don't need glasses at all. I think you never needed them. I think you spent the last several weeks trying to convince your teachers you need glasses, and I know you tried to make something wrong with the test, just so you could get attention from the doctor." Allison felt the emotional 18-wheeler truck slamming into her. She took a deep breath, trying hard to use the shut-down-her-emotions skills she'd developed over the years. She worked hard not to feel the impact of her mother's words.

Then came the statement that would forever change Allison's relationship with her mother.

"I swear to God I should have aborted you."

Allison told me the emotion that flooded her body at that moment was a hurricane for which she was totally unprepared. Her mother's volcanic words were boring into her soul like hot lava. For the first time in her life, she couldn't compartmentalize her mother's verbal attack, and in her anguish asked God right then if there was a way to grant her mother's wish and take Allison out of her body. As her mind raced with images of ending her own life, Allison wished for the courage to make her mother forever live to regret those last words.

The searing pain of her mother's verbal attack stabbed through Allison's heart like a dagger, but this time, Allison told me, something in her snapped. While Allison wished at that moment that her own life was over, it was nothing remotely comparable to the sudden obsession she had with ending her mother's life. Allison could feel in her body that, for the first time, she was truly capable of murdering the human being who had birthed her into this world. This was more than she could take—Allison felt as though her mother had finally trapped her in the emotional cage from which she'd worked so hard to remain free. Allison was overwhelmed with the realization that if she didn't fight to free herself this time, she'd be forever snared in her mother's trap.

Her heart was racing faster than it had ever before, and the anger that flooded her veins completely outweighed the sadness that typically filled her. Allison had been called a liar her entire life, but this time she was going to prove once and for all she was not.

Ship's Engine Blast

Allison sat quietly on the ride home from the doctor's office, her body filled with a rage she'd never experienced before. As usual, Allison's mother had no trouble screaming at the top of her lungs for an extended period of time, but what she didn't know was that her words were fueling Allison's anger—what was coming next was something for which no one could prepare.

By the time Allison and her mother arrived home, Allison could barely see straight. She marched straight to her room—unlike her previous responses to her mother's attacks, she had zero intention of sitting on her floor in a heap, crying herself into a stupor. This time Allison was ready for an act of defiance of which she didn't realize she was capable.

Allison grabbed a drawer from her dresser, dumped the clothes on the floor and let out a blood-curdling scream as she broke the hardwood box in two. She yanked out a second drawer and banged it against the wall until it splintered into little pieces—the force of the banging left a hole the size of a watermelon in the wall. She worked her way through the remaining three drawers, tearing each of them apart, then started on her vanity and night-stands. Her body pulsing with pure adrenaline, she worked her way through each piece of furniture until there was nothing left but a pile of wood, all the while screaming at the top of her lungs. That's when her siblings made their compulsory appearance, standing ready like secret police to report Allison's major infraction.

As they had been taught to do about Allison long ago, her siblings ran immediately to tell Allison's mother about the mess she was making. Allison was so enraged she hadn't the wherewithal to process what was coming for her, but so overtaken was she by her anger that it simply didn't matter—she was determined this time to fight back against her mother's gaslighting with everything she had.

Sure enough, her mother soon slowly materialized at her bedroom door like an apparition manifesting from a foggy mist. In her right hand she gripped a leather belt, pointing it at Allison like a shooter aiming for the kill. Her mother screamed at Allison to end her tirade. Allison glared back at her mother, leaning forward and staring her straight in the eye as if to say, "come and get me." Allison told me that the next words that escaped her lips surprised her—she wasn't cognizant of how much rage filled her until she heard the words with her own ears. She yelled at her mother in a voice she didn't know lived within her. "Fuck you, you crazy bitch! I'm sick of you calling me a liar! I've had it from you—if you're so damn sick of being my mother let's end this shit right now!"

That was all the ammunition Allison's mother needed to release the demon that lived deep inside her. She proceeded to beat her daughter with such force that the belt broke into three pieces before it was over. And as usual, Allison's mother could always count on her three children to help slay the dragon she convinced everyone Allison was—her stockpile of three human weapons braced Allison's arms and legs to the floor, ensuring Allison didn't miss one crack of that thick leather belt against her skin.

Allison did her best to endure the crucifixion laid upon her by her entire family. Despite wishing she possessed the capability to just "give in" to her mother's abusive demands as her siblings had long ago, Allison was born to stand firm against any Goliath in her path. This was by far the most vicious attack she'd ever endured—if this was now the new normal, it was time to abandon ship.

Jumping Ship

In the days following the attack by her mother and siblings, Allison quietly covered up the bruises on her body and kept an extremely low profile both indoors and out. She never spoke about the attack to anyone, and spent the next several days in her home as though nothing had happened. As usual, her mother's extreme manic behavior had slowed for the time being, and she went back to her regular duties as though she was a regular June Cleaver. Her siblings followed suit, retreating to their private worlds of denial as though Allison's recent whipping was no more than two people having a slight difference of opinion.

Allison may have been smart enough to keep a low profile to avoid further confrontation with her mother, but inside her desire to escape was ignited. Though she made a conscious decision at that moment to find the love she was missing from her family, Allison unconsciously spent all her efforts, I discovered, on loving other people even if they were incapable of loving her the same way.

Allison reached out to everyone she knew, pointedly inserting herself into their lives. She became a part of their everyday experiences, and attached herself to as many moms, dads, and siblings of her friends that she knew. Pretty soon she had a group of several families she could turn to for just about anything. She spent increasingly more time away from home, and turned day visits into sleepover nights as often as she could.

Amongst her friends, Allison became the go-to person for getting help with just about anything—boys, girlfriends, homework, and any and all personal problems. Allison was the person her girlfriends leaned on, and they piled their problems onto Allison's shoulders as if she was their very own mythical Atlas. Despite the frustration she sometimes endured from taking on the emotional weight of others, Allison believed it was a small price to pay to be free of her mother—finally, she was liberated.

Lesson Five: Face Rogue Waves Head On

Allison and I continued to talk as we made our way through the Japanese Tea Garden in Golden Gate Park, both of us wiping away tears in between small bites of our salami sandwiches and sips of diet coke. I listened as she spoke more about these "friends" that she believed rescued her from her mother's wrath. What became clear to me is that she'd become so good at managing the problems of others that it seemed "problems" were becoming the only things on which these friendships were based. As I listened to her story, I realized Allison was focusing all her energy on "being a good friend," but these "relationships" kept her from being plugged into her own self-worth.

I listened as she talked about one friend after another, ones that she'd known during her teenage years and others she'd met as an adult. All of these women shared a common denominator—they each proved time and again that Allison was never as important to them as they were to Allison. Most dropped Allison when there was no longer a need to unload emotional baggage. And when Allison tried to share her own worries with the same women she'd helped in the past, they ran for the hills—they were clearly ill-prepared to put in the same problem-solving efforts they demanded from Allison. It seemed that Allison's plan of "over-loving" the people in her life had backfired; she was back to where she was as a child, with no one to love her in the way she deserved.

The more time Allison and I spent delving into her past, the more she came to understand that the only way to heal her pain was to face it head on. Taking on the pain of others purely to compensate for her own deep-seated issues was doing herself a disservice. I shared with Allison that I'd seen this behavior before in other women—they'd spend years burying their emotions in compulsive behaviors that never produced the outcome they sought and eventually became habit. Allison's attempts at using relationships to address her own pain may have at first seemed noble, but in reality she was repeating the same lesson she learned at home—that putting herself last was the key to being human.

Lesson Six: Find the Treasure Within

Now, with years of our "girl-talk-therapy" behind us, I'm proud to say Allison is on the road to recovery. She works hard every day to turn her negative emotions into pathways for regaining her personal power. The emotional abuse she endured as a child left her with layers of self-doubt, egged on by the negative self-talk that played in her head for years. Most important, the abuse left her void of any sense of her own identity, but with lots of time and effort, she's fought hard to get it back.

Allison's biggest challenge was fighting against a power-abuser who came for her innocence. Children are just beginning to build a frame of reference for what constitutes love and respect, and they depend on the first set of human beings they meet in this world to teach them. If that frame is cracked, broken, or destroyed by someone they trust, they are left with no foundation for becoming a healthy human being. I understood why Allison was crying at my family's get-together—in her household, loud voices were a prelude to a having an object thrown at her for just being alive.

What Allison also eventually realized was that she could retain her incredibly kind essence without succumbing to being emotionally bullied. One of the greatest gifts Allison possesses is her ability to love on the highest levels, without terms, conditions, or agenda. She will not cross the line of integrity, and holds herself to the highest standards of humanity. Few people can do that without putting in years of soul work, but Allison was simply born into the world that way.

But these days, before she commits to a relationship of any kind, Allison carefully analyzes how a connection benefits her. She is a firm believer that family and friends of any kind is a privilege, not a right, and that no one is entitled to use familial titles as weapons. The title of mother isn't bestowed upon someone simply because she has a child—it is a title that must be earned through the sharing of mutual love and respect.

Allison's new friends know that she is a light they can look to for help when they are swimming in a dark ocean, but unlike her past relationships, these women stand ready to throw Allison a lifesaver anytime she needs one. Despite what she's been through, Allison knows now that only she owns her soul and spirit, and she continues every day to re-write the chapters of her childhood into the book she always deserved. Allison knows she's no longer required to give up herself to gain love—today, she proudly enjoys all of life's connections as a close first mate and as captain of her own ship.

Seven

DIRTY POOL

*"There's a special place in hell for women
who don't help each other!"*

— MADELINE ALBRIGHT

As difficult as it was to watch Vivian, Claire, and Allison struggle to fully embrace their personal power, it's much worse being the shield that deflects the daggers women throw at one another. Bernadette, Quinn, and Kathleen each came into my life seeking help for hair loss, and their never-ending desire to help other women enduring the same battle moved me constantly. My only wish was that they could have the same love and respect for one another that they had for people they didn't know.

I could count on Bernadette at any time to soothe the anxiousness of a young girl trying to come to grips with her new alopecia diagnosis. As a mother and woman who'd battled hair loss most of her life, Bernadette gave little girls the hope they needed to believe they would not only survive this challenge, they would be better women for it. And for women of every age who couldn't fathom why they were losing the full flowing head of hair they'd known most of their lives, Quinn was their voice of reason, reminding them that their inner strength and willingness to put themselves first made them forever beautiful. Quinn never took no for an answer, and taught the ladies she encountered to do the same. Kathleen was a woman of few words, but her expressions spoke a language all their own. Kathleen's eyes were the windows to her soul, and when women in pain looked into them, they knew her truth. And if they were lucky enough to experience her hugs and the way she gently held the hands of women in need, they'd have all the proof they needed of the kindness that lived within her.

These ladies were my go-to-girls, and I loved them for always being brave enough to let others know they were not alone. Yet as quick as they were to embrace strangers and bestow as much love upon them as necessary, they could be just as prone to treat each other with scorn and offense. The one thing they all had in common was that they each considered themselves to be my "closest friend," and it was that need to have me all to themselves that made them hate each other. To outsiders, each of them appeared to have a genuine love for me, but their constant jockeying for the Queen Bee position almost made any kind of friendship with them unbearable.

Bernadette, Quinn, and Kathleen had so much venomous resentment for each other that I often had to take military-like precautions to be sure they didn't end up in the building at the same time. They each took turns "warning" me about the other every chance they could. Bernadette was determined to make me aware that Quinn's "constant complaining about her life" was such a stressor to me that I needed to "get rid of her" as soon as possible. And the moment Quinn would get me all to herself, she'd talk about how difficult it must be to "be involved with someone like Bernadette," who was "so obnoxious that she didn't deserve you." Kathleen didn't hold back either—though she was the quieter of the three, her scowl whenever Bernadette or Quinn entered the building showed just how much she resented my friendship with them. Her face would be so contorted that she'd completely drain the room of any modicum of happiness.

Besides me, the only thing they had in common was their never-ending quest to win the weight loss war—each of them used the struggle as a weapon on the Queen Bee battlefield. Prepared daily to enact treason against any possible union of sisterhood, they body-shamed each other every chance they could. Bernadette, who was the first of the three women to begin shedding the 30 to 50 pounds they all wanted to lose, salivated over the opportunity to use her liquid diet as a ballistic missile. When she'd come in the door for her appointments with me, she always made sure to shout within earshot of Kathleen and Quinn how much she'd lost this past week.

Her clothes flowed from baggy to form-fitting with every pound she dropped, and she took extra special effort anytime she crossed Kathleen and Quinn in the hallway leading to the shampoo bowls. Bernadette would stop, pull her blouse up to her waist and show off the "jeans I haven't fit into since high school."

I'll never forget the day Bernadette came in for her appointment with her "new look." This once proudly average-size 35-year-old White professional whose choice of dress flowed only between traditional and conservative had transformed to flamboyant, daring, and adventurous. Her previous short, black-bobbed hairpiece was now light-auburn, enhanced with an unapologetic swing bang, and so long it graced the derriere she'd put in hours of dieting to perfect. The glasses she never left home without were now replaced with green contacts so vivid that her eyes came in the room before she did, and the button-down shirts that served as her go-to garments were unabashedly replaced with bustier tops that showed off her newly surgically enhanced breasts.

And the jeans that she'd taken months to fit into? They were yesterday's news. Her new signature look was a tight-fitting mini-skirt that showed off her toned, athletic, "Tina Turner-like" legs. As soon as she'd come in the door, she made sure the conversation turned to the fact that she was now "cute enough to catch a Chippendale's eye," a reference to the fact that she was now frequenting bars and male strip clubs. She made no bones about sitting in the front rows of the strip shows, because she was now "small enough to be picked up by gorgeous, strong, young men and taken for the ride of my life." And this once intensely private woman now had dating profiles all over the Internet.

After she'd driven the weight-loss dagger in far enough, Bernadette, with a voice loud enough for Kathleen and Quinn to hear, invited me to an evening out. As my "best friend," she was always happy to get together, but the invitation meant more when she could throw this one-upmanship in Kathleen and Quinn's faces—not only were she and I going to an event to which they weren't privy, but, at least for now, she was the skinniest person in our group. Bernadette two; Quinn and Kathleen, zero.

Now, as the proprietor of an establishment that celebrates successes of women, I view getting healthy in any capacity as a win for us all. Hell, I've been everything from a size 32 to a size 5, so nobody understands more than I do how it feels to let go of extra weight. But what I can't tolerate is someone using her success as a machete to cut down the self-esteem of another woman who may still be struggling to reach her weight-loss goal.

Lesson Seven: Insecurity is the Storm that Sinks Strong Ships

As much as I wanted to applaud Bernadette's efforts to take control of her health, it saddened me to know they were fuel for hurting other women. Bernadette did everything she could to get the best of others, and the more she displayed this behavior the less I wanted to be a part of her life. I slowly pulled back from Bernadette, making it clear along the way that our relationship was best strictly as client and practitioner—helping Bernadette and watching her help others ensured we always had the best of each other. The sad part is that Bernadette is a woman who can offer so much to so many, but she is so blinded by her insecurity that she won't have the opportunity to experience friendship at its greatest levels. As humans we are by nature flawed creatures— my hope is that one day Bernadette can rise above hers, let go of the jealousy she possesses for women, and let the world see just how great she is.

A Shipload of Self-Absorption

While Bernadette may have been the definition of a closeted hater, Quinn's self-centeredness was in a class by itself. What initially attracted me to Quinn was that in many ways she reminded me of myself. She was one-half of a household of two very successful physicians and thrived when she was able to be a leader. Unlike Kathleen and Bernadette, who struggled with career paths most of their lives and were fighting harder than ever to hold onto their youth, Quinn seemed to be relatively content. She was unquestionably financially independent, fiercely self-reliant, and, even as a married woman, made it clear she answered only to herself. Quinn and I spent a lot of time together—she was my movie date on those rare occasions when I could have time to myself, and we chatted over coffee often about our ongoing responsibilities as professional women. I truly celebrated her success in life, and at one time thought she could be another close friend, someone with whom I could be on equal footing in every way.

As our talks became more personal, Quinn would confide in me how much it hurt to be overweight. This was a subject I understood all too well. Mind you, Quinn never reached the super-obese numbers I once did, but the

30-plus pounds she'd struggled with all her life absolutely infuriated her. She told me in confidence that of all the things she'd achieved in this life, nothing would mean more to her than to squeeze into a mini-skirt, halter top, and six-inch stilettos to become the hottest 40-year-old woman in the room.

She also secretly longed for the envy of other skinny women, who spent years telling her with their eyes that she was too heavy to even dream of being on their levels of physical beauty. Her dream was to one day exact revenge on those very women who perceived her as completely invisible. Though I've never wished to be envied by anyone, I understood what Quinn was trying to tell me. The woman in her longed to be appreciated and told she was beautiful, even if to me she was already one of the most beautiful people I'd known.

So, when Quinn finally took the opportunity to undergo weight-loss surgery, we were both overjoyed, hoping this would be the last straw in her long battle. Naturally I assumed Quinn would keep her weight loss journey private, given all the emotional struggles surrounding her battles with the scale. Instead, as soon as she was approved for surgery, and way before she ever made it to the pre-op consultations, she went on an advertising mission. Quinn announced to everyone with whom she came in contact that "I'm going to be one hundred and ten pounds," whether they asked about it or not. She virtually shoved the information down the throats of anyone who happened to be in the vicinity, because, "I'll be at my goal weight in six months and I just want to make sure you bitches are ready."

Quinn couldn't care less how her words affected others, she just knew she was finally going to be in the Skinny Girl's Club, and she was determined to make damn sure everyone around her knew it. It would be the icing on the cake to the bleached-blond-Marilyn Monroe hair prosthetic she wore to highlight the high cheekbones of her cinnamon-copper-colored Filipina skin and the cherry on top of the new blue contacts she'd chosen exclusively to disguise the brown pupils that never got her the attention she felt she deserved.

She especially took a liking to overwhelming Bernadette with her weight-loss details. By this time, Bernadette had gained back all her weight, plus 50 pounds. Already battling with an underactive thyroid and its corresponding weight-gain and hair-thinning side effects, the liquid diet Bernadette once swore by only made her weight issues worse. When she finally did return to solid food, she put on exorbitant amounts of weight very quickly.

Quinn also knew that Bernadette, who had recently undergone a divorce that left her with only a portion of the financial assets she previously had, did not have the means to afford any kind of bariatric surgery, and Quinn used that to her advantage. Quinn took every opportunity, while in the presence of Bernadette, to discuss every detail of her surgery and how quickly the procedure was going to help her lose the weight once and for all. I felt horrible for Bernadette—she cowered with each comment from Quinn, who gloated that the surgical procedure would soon make it impossible for her to "ever be fat again."

As I was accustomed to doing, I kept the peace between the two using humor and camaraderie. Thank God for my daughter; she had learned from watching me over the years how to smooth out any uneasiness arising amongst clients. I was grateful to have her there to reinforce the comic relief. I focused on the positive, but I couldn't help admitting to myself that the chickens were coming home to roost— Bernadette had been the first to lose weight, and when she did, the hatred she harbored for Quinn and Kathleen oozed out like a festering wound.

Even after re-gaining her weight, Bernadette would constantly tell me Quinn really needed to "get that weight off," and her conversations were rich with name-calling and finger-pointing at other overweight women. It made no sense to me that she could spread so much degradation for women in whose shoes she had so recently walked. And now, Bernadette had to listen to every word Quinn uttered about her own weight loss—Quinn even made sure to rub in that she'd dropped 15 pounds on her own even before surgery.

Lesson Eight: Be the Calm Water in a Flood of Hostility

Witnessing this kind of passive-aggressive bullying between two women I love dearly is so challenging; it wears on my soul and makes my heart cry. I will never forget how being fat made me feel. I'd watched the numbers on the scale crawl upward, and with each bump in digits I'd eat more to manage the pain. I've never had a drink or illicit drug in my life, but for years I dealt with the challenges of my life with sweets, so much so that I was within close range of becoming diabetic. I'd ask myself daily if this was the day my poor eating habits were going to kill me.

I know what it feels like to have eyes boring into me when my back is turned. My life struggles have made it easier to not give two shits what people think or say about me if their only purpose is to sabotage me in some way, but it never felt good knowing my weight may have created an opportunity for me to be disrespected. Particularly in the beauty industry, being fat presents its challenges—here I was encouraging women to be all they could be, but I was letting the weight of my life show on my body. I had to work hard to remain confident despite my weight.

Even when I was gracious, respectful, and inviting when meeting new people, I could read the looks of disgust from skinny women who couldn't imagine being five pounds overweight, let alone my size. And I'd see the anger in the eyes of others—these were the women who happily admitted to me that even though they couldn't compete with my confidence and personal success, at least they weren't fat. I sucked it up and took it like a woman, holding my head high knowing that one day I would live up to my highest vision of myself.

And when I did slowly begin to lose the weight, I tried to prove by example how to treat others. I never had conversations about my weight in public—to me, that's akin to bragging about how much one earns or the car one drives, and I consider this kind of behavior extremely rude and hurtful to others. If a client asked about my weight or complemented me on how much I'd lost, I'd immediately give a compliment right back, reminding the person that "I'm just trying to stay healthy and beautiful like you. Thank you for inspiring me and all women to be healthy." And if she (or he) wanted to know more, I would happily offer to discuss it privately. I'm a woman who's been bald and fat; as such I've had plenty of fingers pointed in my direction. I could never imagine trumpeting my 200-pound weight loss only to make another woman feel small and inadequate.

Besides, envying another woman simply because she was the size I wanted to be was a concept I just didn't know how to entertain. Women to me were beautiful in every size, shape, and color. I celebrated all our uniqueness and embraced the things we had in common. I was a healer by trade and by choice, and the last thing I would ever think to do is use my body, mind, or spirit to harm another woman. So, when I think about the Quinn-and-Bernadette show, I thank God that I'm made the way I am.

I've seen many women siphon the glue from a friendship to feed their own selfish purposes. At no time in a relationship should we allow our own inadequacies to be our weapon against other women. I will never encourage women to embezzle the emotions of their sisters.

Bait and Switch

Bernadette and Quinn's preoccupation with shaming their sisters made me an unwitting witness to the resentment that exists in female relationships, but the "rescue me" game Kathleen wanted me to play at all times made me wish every woman had the insight to know she's her own knight in shining armor. Of the three women, Kathleen—a 45-year-old reserved multiethnic woman whose oversized glasses and short brown hair made her look more like an older librarian than the strong, fit personal trainer she was—she may have been the least outspoken and most laid back, but she was very good at using her reserved demeanor to get her way. Unfortunately, she wasn't prepared for my high emotional quotient—I peeped her game as soon she started to play it.

One weekend during the heyday of our relationship, Bernadette invited me to a party—despite her issues, she was great fun at events and could always make me laugh. Knowing I would have a great time, I brought along Isabel and Kathleen thinking Bernadette would enjoy their company. Anticipating Bernadette's jokes and funny stories, we smiled and laughed all the way to the party. It's when we met Bernadette at the door that I realized I'd made a terrible mistake bringing Kathleen.

I'll never forget the way Bernadette looked at Kathleen when I introduced them to each other. Trying her hardest to hide the scowl, Bernadette wasn't even able to shake hands with the woman, lest her rage at someone else being with "her Helen" take over. Instead of welcoming her with open arms, which Bernadette knows is what I would expect, Bernadette stared at Kathleen with such hostility that if looks could kill, Kathleen would have lost an eyeball that night. After what seemed like an eternity, the only thing Bernadette was able to muster was, "I don't really know what to say. I trust no one, especially with you, Helen. These people are always trying to attach themselves to something." Bernadette said this out loud. Straight to Kathleen's gobsmacked face. Then she turned on her heel and abruptly walked away.

At first, I was surprised at how quickly Kathleen seemed to let it go, but then I realized Kathleen had quickly done the math in her head—she saw the look on Bernadette's face and knew instantly that Bernadette was jealous of her. As Kathleen made her way into the party and introduced herself to a few people, I could see she'd come up with her own equation. "Helen picked me up to go to Bernadette's party, so I must be at least as important as Bernadette, this woman she's known for years. I rode in with Helen and Isabel so you know I'm family; I didn't even have to drive my own car. It's official. Helen is my new best friend. And this bitch can't do a damn thing about it."

Once I did the same math, I knew I might have to put on my Wonder-Woman-bullet-deflecting bracelets in case these two got into it. But Kathleen handled herself more than gracefully, introducing herself to everyone and dancing the night away. We all had a fabulous evening and laughed about it on the way home.

It wasn't until the next day that things got ugly—that's when I realized Kathleen's mental equation had only one solution: Me. In her mind, the party was her invitation into every aspect of my life.

Kathleen's first foray into thinking I was now her possession was to invite me to her house for lunch. Seemed outwardly harmless, but I knew she was slowly weaving her web. Kathleen had seen with her own eyes the number of people who approached, trusted, and looked up to me. This intrigued her; she had "never seen someone so popular before." Later, privately, she took my hand, looked me straight in the eye, and with all the sarcasm she could muster, told me how "honored she was to have a friend like me." That was this damsel's first cry of distress, and I knew some level of passive-aggressive behavior wasn't far behind.

I started spending more time with Kathleen and learning more about her life. Like all the women before her, she came into my life looking for help, and there seemed no harm in sharing a little time with a woman in search of some small level of fulfillment. As a three-time divorcee with no children, Kathleen lived a quiet life with her cats. In the beginning, I enjoyed spending time with her—her quiet life gave me respite and relaxation and her cats melted my Fur Mommy heart every time I saw them.

It's when I started to get busy with work that things really changed. Kathleen would text me in the middle of the day, looking for me to join her for lunch, and when I explained that it just wasn't in the cards this week, she'd politely text back that she understood but then follow up with, "What about next week?" Whenever I declined, I would be sure to let her know I loved her and would be thinking of her, but that I didn't want my crazy schedule to keep her from other activities. She would send me a thumbs-up or smiley face emoji to let me know she understood. I'm thinking, we're good.

When I finally did get some time to go and visit her, she was at first somewhat aloof. I thought maybe she was a bit tired, so I made small talk with her for a while until she felt comfortable enough to open up. That's when the ugly-cry commenced. She proceeded to tell me through swollen eyes and a waterfall of tears that I must be mad at her because I couldn't make time to see her. I tried hard to let her vent, but couldn't help the frustration that arose in me. I quietly let her know that it was nothing personal, I just could not get time away from work. She continued her tantrum, repeating that I couldn't be the friend she thought I was unless I could make time to get together. I listened as she vented about all the things I was doing wrong that made her feel like she wasn't good enough to be my friend. I tried to console her, reminding her that just because I couldn't be with her all the time didn't mean I didn't love and appreciate her as a person.

Eventually she calmed down, and I gave her a big hug to let her know she was special to me. But I also made a mental note that it was time to back away from this one. Kathleen needed someone to rescue her, and I was not in a position to carry her on my back. I had hoped that just having someone to talk to at times would be helpful to her, but clearly that wasn't enough.

I started to sense later that she was beginning to resent me. In her mind, if she could guilt me into spending more time with her, she'd get the attention she wanted, on her terms.

Eventually I left Kathleen alone altogether. She moved on soon thereafter, finding new friends to hang out with and taking on a new business venture with a dear friend. Good for her. I was proud of her; being brave enough to find and understand her own true purpose in life was a first step in learning to undo her compulsion to guilt others into loving her.

Lesson Nine: Cruise with the Right Crew

I refuse to encourage women to compete with other women's strengths, hearts, or successes. Vivian wanted to use her beauty and her men to make other women feel inadequate and insubstantial. Claire used her relationship with money to target strong women and hold them emotionally accountable for her own life-choices. Allison, who has a lifelong track record of outwardly supporting her sisters, once believed she had to sacrifice her inner sister to survive in this world. Bernadette and Quinn created an intense, body-shaming rivalry solely to bring pain and suffering to their fellow sisters still struggling with weight issues. And Kathleen used her passive-aggressive skills to rope women into her world, just so she could avoid dealing directly with her own personal issues.

Each of these women failed to recognize that as women, they have a host of gifts to bring to the tables of sisterhood. Instead they set out to break those tables in half and leave their sisters nowhere to sit. I can only imagine where Bernadette and Quinn would be in their weight-loss goals if they'd supported one another instead of tearing each other down. If Claire had taken more pride in her life's accomplishments instead of making excuses for what she didn't have, she would be exchanging ideas daily at a table of amazing, powerful women. And if Vivian and Kathleen had been as focused on handling their own lives as they were on searching for someone else to carry their emotional loads, they, too, would be proudly seated with their sisters. Allison continues her quest to empower other women, but she must always remember that to be a good sister, her inner sister must always come first.

I'm convinced that by using our strengths to build alliances with our sisters, rather than using our perceived hatred of one another to divide us, we become forces to be reckoned with. Each of us has borne witness to our own unique pain and suffering. We can use that to empathize with our sisters and be the great love in their lives that each of us hopes one day to experience.

One thing I've always known how to do is to be a good friend, and to that end I will only allow love and respect to be fostered in my environment. What Vivian, Claire, Bernadette, Quinn, and Kathleen all have in common is that they aren't willing to leave their selfish love behind for a love that envelops equally each person it touches. I can only wonder why some of my ladies, who are already undergoing personal challenges and battling painful disorders and illnesses, don't want to take advantage of the warmth and experience that other women can provide them. Instead, they see other women as a threat. Women possess an innate ability to love on the highest levels; we need to exercise that love with our most important allies—other women.

I encourage as many women as I can to be a friend to themselves, and therefore become a true friend to others. Whenever I have this discussion with Allison, she always has the same answer. "Go ahead," she says, "Analyze our friendship as often, and through as many lenses as you need. Because a true friend will always prove herself friendly and is too busy being a real friend to worry about you finding out she's not."

Eight

SERENITY FOR SISTERS WHO SAIL THE SAVAGE SEAS

"Sisterhood is powerful."

– KATHIE AMATNIEK SARACHILD

My life aspirations have led me into communities far and wide, affording me the opportunity to engage with women of different races, classes, ages, and religions. When I meet a woman, my first instinct is to assess where she's been in her life, and then do whatever I can to let her know I embrace her. That usually leads to a physical embrace, my way of showing what each of these women mean to me.

As a stylist, I've worked with women from every lifestyle—public and private. The rainbow of colorful women in my chair at any given time is a clear reflection of this, and my clients welcome the opportunity to connect with women of every facet of society. Still, as a Black female stylist, there are some occasions when I'm pulled aside by African-American patrons because they're unfamiliar with salons that also serve non-Black women. It never ceases to amaze me to witness the look of disbelief that comes across their faces when they see a Caucasian woman come through the door. They whisper through clenched teeth, as though an act of pure blasphemy has just been committed.

"Girl, you do White women in here?" As I laugh and help them to get comfortable with the idea, I let them know I understand their concerns.

Though each of our establishments is unique, the African-American Hair Salon for many Black women is as sacred a space as the Black Church. It's where we allow ourselves to be all of who we are, sharing our grievances, and celebrating our triumphs. It's also the one place where we feel our unique hair types are understood. For that reason, it's important I acknowledge our shared experiences as African-American women. But I also share the joy of being able to unite a diverse group of women of racial backgrounds, economic strata, and sexual orientations. We are women of all cultures, colors, ideas, and opinions, yet we have all come together in search of answers to our unique illnesses and conditions. To that end, we often have more in common than we realize. I understood this lesson in childhood when I learned that angels often come in the packages we least expect.

Directing My Own Vessel

Growing up in the projects means you have to get clear very quickly on who you're going to be. You're either going to be the bullied kid, the kid who bullies others, or the one that stands up against bullying altogether. What I remember most about my mostly Black neighborhood was how much the kids wanted to fight. They wanted to fight me, they wanted to fight each other, and they wanted to fight their elders and anyone else they could find. Most of them even fought with themselves—the anger they carried reflected the lack of hope in their communities. For many in my neighborhood, fighting was the only way to feel worthy; fighting gave these kids power to be "something" against the "nothing" they faced every day.

I hated fighting, but I could handle myself if the situation called for it. For one girl who hated me, cornering me every day after school was the highlight of her day. I tried daily to let her know I wouldn't fight her, but my coordinated Montgomery Ward and Sears-catalog school clothes, the scent of the Charlie perfume that floated behind me as I walked, and my unabashed determination to make proper use of the English language were all too much for her. She thought she was going to teach me a lesson about "acting so damn White." I managed to keep her at bay for a while, but she eventually attacked me. She was in for a surprise—I hit that girl so hard she stumbled several steps and took a small tumble before hitting the pavement. I used the time she took to collect herself to make my way to the school parking lot. Little-Miss-Asshole-with-the-Big-Ass-Attitude never bothered me again.

Sailing toward Sisterhood

What I also remember about that fight was that my only rescuers were two girls who looked nothing like me and knew nothing of my experience. Unlike the girl who hated me for having the audacity to want more for my life than what was expected of kids like me, these two girls—White biological sisters who lived in one of the wealthiest communities of San Francisco—embraced me as one of their own. Though they couldn't be in the streets of my community to break up the daily fist fights, or accompany me on the bus ride home to shield me from the cursing and name calling that was considered normal for kids in my neighborhood, what they did do was make sure I knew they were my friends.

I met The Sisters the year I was bused to the Diamond Heights district, a quiet community near Noe Valley that bordered several other desirable, family-oriented residential areas. Though I was too young to fully comprehend the political implications of busing and school desegregation, I did understand that the majority-Black schools in my neighborhood had much less and were much more impoverished than other schools in the City. I also understood that like many cities, economics had created a Mason-Dixon line between the wealthy and the poor that separated many families of color from their White counterparts. When the opportunity came for me to attend school in a more economically advantaged neighborhood, I happily accepted the offer—even as a child I wanted to explore every opportunity that might lead a path toward success.

I remember the first day the school bus took me across town—I noticed right away how much the neighborhoods changed. The blocks of graffiti-lined walls and trash-littered sidewalks of my neighborhood were replaced by the perfectly manicured lawns of St. Francis Wood and well-maintained buildings in Glen Park that looked like they'd just had a fresh coat of paint. The run-down apartments with iron-rod barred windows to which I was accustomed gave way to pristinely modernized Noe Valley Victorians and upscale, suburban Diamond Heights single-family homes. The best part of being in Diamond Heights for a six-plus-hour school day was that no one wanted to fight.

For the most part, I made plenty of friends there, but it was my visits with The Sisters that gave me the energy to hope for a life beyond the neighborhood in which I lived. Though they could have their pick of any exclusive or private schools in their neighborhood, The Sisters' parents preferred the active move toward diversity and the progressive, well-rounded education of the Diamond Heights schools. I was invited to their home every day after school, and from the back seat of their mother's freshly washed-and-waxed Mercedes Benz, I took in every ounce of the panoramic views as we made our way into their affluent neighborhood. As I looked out at the large homes that lined these streets and watched children play with their new toys in their spotless front yards, I could see my future. Though I was proud of who I was and where I came from, I knew that I had the potential for more.

Being with The Sisters not only provided welcome relief from the turbulent bus ride home I'd be forced to endure later in the day, it helped me learn to make plans for solidifying the future of my dreams. Though they had exponentially more than I did, they were kind to me and made sure I wanted for nothing during the time we spent together.

Their bedrooms were painted in beautiful pink pastels, and I felt like Cinderella every time I entered and saw the small bottles of Faberge shampoos and Avon perfume samples that sat atop their matching chest of drawers and vanity. I had no shortage of toys to play with any time I'd visit. They had porcelain dolls from every corner of the world, dolls that could talk simply by pulling a string and dolls that could "pee" when fed with their coordinating small plastic bottles. My favorites were the southern-belle-inspired figurines—their sculpted, delicate faces were enhanced by peaches-and-cream colored makeup and adorned with pink, lilac, and indigo doll-size evening gowns with matching bonnets and parasols. Their closets held a wardrobe fit for a queen and had stacks of board games that could keep us busy for hours.

This was especially great for days when the always-cold San Francisco weather would turn to rain. We spent our afternoons spinning the wheel in the game of Life, mesmerized by the geometric shapes of rotating Spirograph pieces, or disagreeing over who deserved to be the "wheelbarrow" in this day's Monopoly game. We had plenty of options and lots of fun.

I'd spend hours rifling through the pink vinyl storage cases that housed their vast Barbie collection. The Sisters quickly designated me as "master decorator" of Barbie's Dream House, thanks to the artistic eye and manual dexterity I inherited from my painter father. They realized I had a knack for putting the tiny furniture in just the right places to make the dollhouse appear inviting. And they loved to see me race through "onesies, twosies, and threesies" in the game of Jacks; they'd watch in awe as I hit "pigs-in-a-pen" minutes after the game started. The house was always quiet and peaceful, and sometimes I could hear the "Swan Lake music," as one of my siblings called it, emanating from their mother's hi-fi stereo through the marble floored and columned-lined halls of their home. The sweet sounds of those classical melodies immediately put me at ease.

One thing I remember very well was being able to eat whatever snacks I wanted, without worrying that there wouldn't be enough for us all. I remember eyeing the pantry when I followed one of the girls into the kitchen to grab a glass of water. I was almost in shock when I noticed there was an entire closet available just for food storage. It was like looking inside a grocery store. This wasn't just a few shelves in a cabinet that held a couple of cans of beans or ravioli. This was a full walk-in space, completely filled with every imaginable culinary refreshment. There were cookies of every variety, cupcakes and fruit pies in every flavor, and sodas and bottled drinks that went way beyond the little packages of Kool-Aid to which I was accustomed. This would be one time I wouldn't have to listen to someone shouting about "eating up all the food in the house," a line I heard almost daily as my mother tried hard to ration what little food she could afford amongst her six children. My mother once admitted to me that there were days she'd endured insurmountable abdominal pain from not eating, just so she would have enough food on hand to feed her children. It was clear The Sisters didn't have to worry about things like this, and I'd felt like I'd just hit the Food Lottery. Knowing I could have anything in this space that I wanted was almost overwhelming, and I couldn't help but wonder what it would be like for our family if we had this much food at home every day. I think the sister I was with that day must have seen the excitement in my eyes, because her mother came into her bedroom a few minutes later with a plate of the very snacks I'd been eyeing.

The Sisters' Mom would come in and check on us every so often to see if we needed anything. This, too, was a completely unfamiliar concept to me. My mother spent all her available time at work, and my opportunity to spend "quality" time with her came when I'd pop in to see her at her waitressing job. She'd fix me a plate that she paid with using her tips, and I was grateful for a full meal. In return I'd help her out a bit, grabbing a few of her orders and taking them to her customer's tables. I'd smile as I introduced myself as her daughter, and her customers would praise my mother for raising such a kind child. We took time to enjoy each other's company, even if it meant we had to work through it. It was lovely to see The Sisters enjoy the opportunity to be raised by a mother who could afford to stay home, and seeing them together made me appreciate my mother's hard work even more.

The more time I spent with The Sisters, the clearer it became to me that there was a road to freedom from the meager employment opportunities, limited educational opportunities, and the depression and overall lack of hope that permeated my neighborhood. As our childhood friendship grew, The Sisters would turn my daytime visits into sleepover nights. The after-school snacks I received at their house eventually graduated to in-school lunches their mother would pack for me from time to time, and send to me at school through her daughters. I kept the fact that I was being fed by this family a secret from my mother. Even though I knew in some way my mother would appreciate the kind gesture, I understood that no woman who is struggling daily to feed her family wants to be singled out as a charity case. My mother and her children may not have had much, but we were proud of what we did have.

The Sisters were especially supportive of me when I started to lose my hair, never once commenting on my receding hairline or pointing out the obvious bald patches on my head. I couldn't count on the same respect from kids in my own neighborhood, who took every opportunity to remind me that I was "bald-headed" after noticing my efforts to assemble parts of my mother's worn-out wigs into some kind of wearable hairpiece. I'd often get a little pit in the bottom of my stomach every time the clock struck 4:30pm while at The Sisters' house; I knew that meant it was time for me to start making my way back home.

Lesson Ten: Love Is the Wind in Your Sails

Mormon Church official Carl Buehner once said, "They may forget what you said, but they will never forget how you made them feel." What The Sisters taught me was that White people were not the threatening, untrustworthy "blue-eyed devils" some people in my Hunter's Point neighborhood were convinced they were. So fearful were some of my neighbors that they would lock their doors and windows and scream a warning to other Black neighbors that White people were present. But these two White girls helped shape my vision of reality—they were proof that love comes in many packages and stands in solidarity with those it embraces. The Sisters came to my emotional rescue while those who looked like me only brought me pain and suffering. We were from two very different worlds, but in my eyes The Sisters were every bit of my family. What these two beautiful little girls brought me was love, and love always wins.

Nine

THE MANY COLORS OF THE DEEP BLUE SEA

"And then Alek Wek came onto the international scene;
she was dark as night and everyone was talking about
how beautiful she was. I wanted to reject it because
I'd begun to enjoy the seduction of inadequacy."

— *LUPITA NYONGO*

When I share my childhood story of The Sisters with women—Black, White, or of any ethnicity—my choice to live an all-inclusive life makes sense. As an African-American woman and child of the Civil Rights movement, I'm reminded that segregation would have at one time made it impossible for me to provide services for women of any other ethnicity but my own. And I'm even more thankful to be living in an environment where I can celebrate the hair of all my sisters, given that at one point in our early American history, Tignon Law[1] forbade Black women from exposing their natural hair in public. I've always said that hair loss doesn't discriminate; it

---

1 Tignon Law prescribed and enforced appropriate public dress for African American women in the late 1700s. Passed under the administration of Louisiana Governor Esteban Rodriguez Miro, Tignon Law ensured African American women covered their hair and heads with a knotted headdress and refrained from excessive attention to dress so as not to compete with White women for attention from White men and threaten the social order.

strikes women and girls of all ages, races, ethnic groups, and socio-economic backgrounds. Rather than separate from our sisters based solely on skin color, I've found that we all heal much faster by supporting one another and sharing our common experiences. When I'm with my ladies of any color, I am a beautiful African-American woman, celebrated both for my uniqueness and my common love for my sisters. When we come together to heal one another, there is simply no room, nor interest, in dissecting the hue of my skin tone. In the world of inclusiveness, women of all colors are beautiful.

I often wonder if I could teach some of the women in my old neighborhood these same ideas. I wish I could let them know that they are beautiful, and that their complexion does not define their paths to success. In an all-encompassing world, women of all colors are beautiful.

I will always foster an environment of inclusiveness in my practice, but I'm also aware that many of us hail from communities that teach us to believe our propensity for success is based on skin tone. Particularly in densely populated African-American neighborhoods like the one in which I was raised, we may be segmented into color categories that can weigh heavily on our ability to believe in our goals and aspirations. So intensely driven into our communities is this colorism idea that it succeeds in stifling many from recognizing their own worth. When I think about Little Miss Asshole, I can only wonder if the rage she projected onto me was not only driven by her frustration over her life circumstances, but also secretly embedded in the variation of our respective skin tones.

It may seem strange, but it's almost sometimes easier to fight the institutionalized and systemic racism in the world at large than to battle the "light-skinned, dark-skinned" war that rages within my community.

Blurred Vision in Murky Waters

My daughter Isabel is a beautiful chocolate-mocha color, with intense dark-brown eyes and voluptuous full lips. My son Aaron, slender with a perfect muscular build and brown-hazel eyes, was so light at birth people thought I was his nanny. I also have siblings who range the gamut of colors. As far as I was concerned, we've always been one big, rainbow-colored family.

What I did learn later was that colorism ran further in my family and my surroundings than I realized at the time, but I was so driven to leave my surroundings where poor and hopelessness was the norm that I didn't have time to pay attention to such useless banter. Becoming a teenage mother forced me to grow up quickly, so my only focus at that time was trying to figure out how I was going to feed my kids.

When I did have opportunities to talk with my mother about growing up in the Jim Crow South, she shared memories of watching her lighter-skinned cousins boldly enter White-only restaurants to enjoy the specials of the day without worry—their yellow-hued complexions and light eyes made the owners and patrons assume they were as White as them. And her stories of having to walk to school and church while her lighter-skinned relatives were driven in the family car made me hurt for the segregation my mother experienced.

As I processed the impact of her stories, I thought more about some of the comments I used to hear from Black people when I rode the city buses with my two kids. I remember hearing things like, "Your son is so much lighter than you; he must have a White father." Or, "Your daughter is so pretty even though she is darker than you." Smiling strangers would come up to me ready to dote on my two babies. But once they noticed my daughter was the darker skinned of the two, the attention would immediately turn to my son. I didn't put together that they were responding to his color until I was older.

And when my kids started noticing that they were "lighter" or "darker" I was dumbfounded. I couldn't understand where this was coming from since I never made this an issue at home. But Isabel would later confide in me that as a little girl she wished she was closer in color to her mother. Other Black children called her "big-lips" and "darkie" at school. The White children, on the other hand, constantly complimented her on her skin tone, hairstyles, and personality—I remember that with a few exceptions Isabel was often the only Black child at her sleepovers and birthday parties.

When I'm surrounded by women who've been made to believe their worth is defined by color, I remind them that feelings of inadequacy only fester when we've been persuaded to believe we are powerless. The great Martin Luther King once said, "A man can't ride you unless your back is bent." In my world, a woman stands tall and tenacious, and the only things riding her back are determination and fearlessness.

A Wave of Uncertainty in an Ocean of Color

Annabelle came into my life as a young woman, vibrant, full of life, and ready to take on the world. Annabelle had big dreams—she wanted a house on the hill, a fancy job title with a fancier salary, and the perfect designer bag and heels to reinforce all that she'd accomplished. She was just 18, but believed her dreams weren't too far from becoming reality. She was sprinting through life with joy and vitality, reminding me of all the hopes and dreams I had for myself.

Annabelle's interest in my services was twofold. She was in search of a specialist who could assist her in managing a lifelong compulsive disorder that resulted in her unique hair loss condition. But she also wanted to work with someone who could help her retain her youthful looks while helping her fight this one-of-a-kind ailment. I understood this idea completely—the one reward I received from losing my hair was the ability to create and wear extraordinary, one-of-a-kind hair prosthetics that always made a statement. Annabelle wanted a head full of long, flowing, youthful tresses that could reflect the "woman-at-the-top" vision she had for herself. She was on board from the moment I started brainstorming her design—Annabelle was determined that the scars on her scalp and the bald patches that breached her limited follicles would not break her bond with her womanhood. Right on, sister, I thought. Do your thing.

Annabelle not only celebrated her femininity with confidence, but she was also one of the most striking women I'd ever seen. As an African-American woman, I am more than familiar with the variations in hue and tone that women of our race are fortunate to enjoy, and Annabelle was a true reflection of that beauty. Her complexion was a velvety-smooth shade of blue-black that commanded whatever room she was in and glistened when she was in the sunshine. Her pearly-white teeth gave way to a perfect smile whenever she laughed, and her smile only further softened her milky skin.

She was breathtaking. And she knew it. I must admit that even in my youth I wasn't the girl that men pushed past to meet other women, but Annabelle was such a vision that anyone present with her automatically became invisible. Men of every race stopped in their tracks when they saw her coming. As her healer and mentor, I enjoyed watching the attention she received. It reminded me that my work was helping to bring out the absolute best in my client, and this was something I always celebrated, even if it meant the men were looking past me to get to her. I felt my chest inflate with pride; I loved this baby girl like a daughter, and I was so proud to see her shine.

Annabelle's confidence appeared to be so strong outwardly that I was sure this was the one client of mine who would be an amazing resource for other women. I played out the myriad scenarios in my head constantly, all of them involving Annabelle popping in to my consultation rooms to share her stories of perseverance and pizazz, giving hope to other women who were struggling to find their way back to themselves. I would soon come to learn, however, that as one of her colleagues later whispered to me, Annabelle "was not what she appeared to be."

Since childhood, Annabelle had been told by both her Black and White acquaintances that she was pretty. With a look that was so unique it couldn't be pigeonholed, Annabelle could not simply be categorized as "dark" or "light." To her community, she was a fascinating multicultural blend, an exquisite, exotic package that transcended color. I can think of a thousand women who would have given their right arm to have their beauty worshipped this way.

Annabelle, however, had a completely different idea of what it meant to receive this kind of attention. She soon realized she could use her unique beauty as a method for oppressing other women.

During one of her appointments with me, Annabelle admitted that she truly hated her skin color. She didn't simply dislike, or sometimes feel a bit uncomfortable in her own skin, but unequivocally hated her pigment with a passion. What's interesting is that Annabelle never experienced the kind of name-calling and put-downs that other dark-skinned girls around her reported enduring, so the self-hate she lived with everyday wasn't a result of outside influence. In fact, Annabelle's experience was just the opposite—she'd been told most of her life that she was incredibly beautiful.

She was never subjected to the "brown-paper-bag" insults aimed at dark-hued women, and never experienced hearing references to "darky" or "smoky," words my own child and her darker-skinned friends reported hearing. She never had any compulsion to accuse light-skinned women of "having it easy," or "acting White." Annabelle was the definition of beauty, something every woman she encountered longed to be. Yet she hated everything about the body in which she lived.

Annabelle's self-hate was manifested in her desire to always be the center of attention. She wanted to make sure no one else could be on equal footing, and she interpreted my spending time with other women I cared for as a direct threat. Even spending time with my own daughter was a threat. She was most comfortable when men were fighting over her and women were fighting with her. She did whatever she could to introduce chaos into calm situations. Regardless of how many people told her she was beautiful, it wasn't enough. She not only needed to hear constantly that she was pretty, she also needed to make sure she heard it in front of other women. This allowed her to convince herself that these women were jealous of her beauty, thereby making her feel empowered. Her entire world revolved around the fact that she was the "dark one" of her family, and the "darkest one" wherever she went—she was so full of inadequacy about her skin color that she vied for control of everyone around her, especially me.

Rather than admit to herself that she needed to address her self-hate, Annabelle preferred to pounce on the confidence of other women and blame them for her emotional distress. Each time I saw her she'd announce how many men had ogled her that day. Annabelle took every opportunity to drive home the fact that she could command more attention in the room than anyone. Her hatred of her skin tone was just as categorically clear as the fact that her confidence masked her own self-loathing.

My theory was proven correct one night when Allison, Isabel, Annabelle, and I went out to a party. Annabelle wore a revealing teddy that hugged her size-two body and pushed her $10,000 breasts up to her chin. She made it a point to swing her hair extensions around coyly every time a man entered the room. She was fully prepared to "slay" all the women in the room—I tried to keep from rolling my eyes every time I looked at her and just have fun with my friends and family.

About 20 minutes into our time at the party, a slim young Caucasian man asked a smartly-dressed, African-American, plus-size woman to dance. Though she had just sat down to have a drink she gladly accepted. By the time we all noticed her, she was tearing up the dance floor—Sis could move, and she had all eyes on her. Two of the guy's friends decided to join in, and pretty soon she was leading them all across the dance floor. I watched her run the room, smiled, and clapped my hands right along with her. She was confident, self-assured, and was handling her business. You go girl.

Annabelle, on the other hand, could barely contain herself. For the first time in a long time, someone else—a dark-skinned, plus-size woman—was getting more attention than her. We weren't at the party more than an hour before she started sulking and begging me to take her home. I knew exactly what the problem was—Annabelle was on the verge of a temper tantrum—but I wasn't about to take my guests home. We stayed for a several more hours, danced with men and women alike, and had a beautiful time bonding. I could only hope at that moment Annabelle was learning that self-love is one of the greatest gifts we can give ourselves.

Lesson Eleven: An Ocean View Comes with Vivid Colors

As with many of the women who come into my life in a state of emotional flux, Annabelle eventually drifted on to the next stage of her life. I think she finally figured out that no matter how much she tried, I wasn't going to give up my family and friends to satisfy her ego. My world has always consisted of showering as much love as I can on women of every race and economic opportunity—Annabelle quickly learned I would not allow her to sabotage the kindness I fostered on many, nor would I allow the kindness of others to be damaged by her emotional baggage. This was a lesson in self-hate she would have to overcome on her own.

It's been years since I've seen her, but my truest hope for Annabelle is that she learns to embrace herself for all she is—mind, body, soul, and spirit. I can only imagine the lessons in acceptance and tolerance Annabelle could have taught us all if she had loved herself from the start.

Today, when I hear discussions about skin color, I firmly put my foot down if the conversation draws negative comparisons between light and dark complexions. I remind my ladies that it's our unique hues that make us who we are. Our skin color, just like the hair on our heads, may present us with challenges, but when we are empowered, the stigmas others place upon us are removed. I remind my sisters that it's up to each of us to know our hearts and souls are sacred, and in knowing our power, we are capable of living as the greatest versions of ourselves.

Ten

STAYING AFLOAT IN ROUGH WATERS

"Don't let money rule you."

— THE O'JAYS

My best friend Allison says that we teach others how we want to be treated by the way we carry ourselves. I firmly believe that. I'm especially moved when I'm working with women struggling to treat themselves well. Already in private battles with hair by the time they come to see me, my clients are all too often also battling physical illness. Sometimes it takes everything they've got just to get out of bed.

But after years of doing restorative work on women's hair, I've learned that if the soul is strong, it can help weaken the effects of whatever ailment troubles the body. My ladies and I employ whatever techniques are needed to uplift one another—sometimes that's prayer, sometimes it's a good laugh, and sometimes it's just taking a quiet moment to hold each other. And when we are empowered, we can face head-on any challenge that comes our way.

It's so important to me that my ladies use all available tools at their disposal to help discover, hold onto, or regain all of who they are. When I see the women for whom I care confronting any emotional battle, I'm ready to draw my sword and let them know they are not alone.

But I've also learned my belief in another woman's success isn't enough unless she herself believes in her power to succeed. Take Samantha, a friend of Allison and a woman with great promise. Samantha and Allison had known each other since they were kids and spent most of that friendship doing what they could to support one another. Given Allison's turbulent home life, Samantha was one of the first people in Allison's life who showed Allison she mattered. When Allison was with Samantha, she was free of the judgment and put-downs disguised as love she was subjected to at home. She was free of the name-calling and belt-beatings her mother considered a necessary part of child-rearing. She was free of the constant screaming and finger-pointing she and her siblings received simply for offering an opinion. With Samantha, she was free to be herself.

Samantha did everything from encouraging Allison's personal expression to making sure she had cards and gifts on her birthdays and at Christmas. Simple acts of kindness like these were something Allison never experienced at home, and Allison eventually learned that "friendship," "love," and "family" didn't have to be tainted with pain and suffering. Meeting Samantha helped Allison learn to trust someone again. But as Allison tells it, she would have not as easily offered up her trust if she knew at the time what it would cost to be Samantha's friend.

The Quiet Storm

One Sunday, Allison was making her way home to the condominium she and Samantha shared. Allison and Samantha stayed close after high school and met up a few years into adulthood to rent a snazzy home in Silicon Valley. Samantha was out with her boyfriend for the day, and this was one of those days Allison couldn't wait to get in the door—she'd had to work all weekend and was looking forward to a few hours of relaxation before Monday morning rolled around. This Sunday was also her birthday, and after giving up her off days she wanted only to celebrate by resting quietly at home.

Allison was about five minutes away from her house when she thought about running one final errand before heading home. "I should probably go to the dry cleaner and pick up my laundry," she thought to herself. She kept driving, thinking that didn't make sense. She knew of not one dry cleaner in America that would be open on a Sunday. She pressed on ahead, practically drooling over the thought of getting out of her close-fitting work clothes and into her favorite pair of pajamas.

That's when she heard her inner voice again, but this time it was louder. "Allison, you really need to head to the dry cleaner." Again, she argued with the voice, telling it that the place wouldn't be open and therefore it made zero sense to turn around. Plus, Allison had recently been having car trouble. She knew if she stopped and parked she might have trouble getting the vehicle to start again. Undeterred, she pressed on.

The voice came through again, and this time it was a thundering, ear-splitting command. Allison was now less than 300 feet from her house. "ALLISON! GO TO THE DRY CLEANER RIGHT NOW!" the voice demanded. Allison told me when she heard the voice this time, she immediately made a U-turn and made a beeline for the dry cleaner. She parked the car, leapt out, and ran to the door just to see if by some chance it was open. Just as she thought, the store was closed on Sundays. And just as she'd predicted, her car wouldn't start once she'd parked it. It took over three hours for a tow truck to arrive to Allison's aid, and she didn't make it home until well after dark. But she was not in any way prepared for what she saw when she arrived.

Mayday!

As Allison put her key in the front door, she noticed it was ajar. Her first thought was that Samantha must have just arrived home, so she came inside and called out to her. No answer. She walked upstairs, calling out Samantha's name, thinking she was in her bedroom and didn't hear her. Still, no answer.

Allison slowly opened Samantha's bedroom door to peek inside. It was at that moment that she saw it. Broken glass littered Samantha's carpet and bed, and the bedroom window that was still intact was wide open. In that instant, it hit her—if Allison had not stopped at the dry cleaner she would have walked into a robbery that could have turned into something much worse. The police would later find the fingerprints of three or four assailants on the window—there's no doubt in my mind Allison could have lost her life that day if she'd arrived home even a moment earlier.

I thank God every day that Allison made the choice to do the opposite of what so many women do—they ignore their intuition and inner voice, and in so doing inevitably regret it. Countless women have told me they wish they'd "listened to themselves" and made decisions they knew in their hearts were right but didn't have the courage to accept.

Allison chose to heed the warnings of the voice inside her, and it saved her life. But her willingness to hear the message also led her to a painful conclusion. Allison learned shortly after the robbery that her house was not burglarized at random. In fact, it was because of her relationship with Samantha that her life could have been sacrificed.

About six months before they agreed to rent their condominium together, Allison met up with Samantha and her then-boyfriend Max for dinner. Allison would later confide in me that she felt uncomfortable with Max the minute they were introduced—Samantha had casually mentioned to Allison prior to the meetup, as if it were no big deal, that Max had spent time in prison but that he "was reformed and deserved another chance." As a child of two drug-addicted parents who were in prison for robbery and attempted murder and raised from the age of three by three sets of foster parents, Samantha had made it adamantly clear to Allison that she wanted nothing to do with the "bad-boy lifestyle." But Samantha was convinced that Max was a changed man and wanted to give him a chance to rectify his past. She said it was only fair she gave him "the same chance my foster parents gave me." So Allison reluctantly went along and, out of respect for the friendship, tried to have an open mind.

Yet Allison found Max incredibly difficult to tolerate—Max spent most of the evening rolling his eyes whenever Allison spoke, convinced that she was using her "big words" as a put-down directed at him. Max was convinced that Allison thought she was "better than him" and later admitted it to Samantha. Allison told me she'd always kept in mind that strong women can be a threat to weak-minded people, but that she was still willing to try and be friendly toward Max. She waited it out, hoping Samantha would soon come to her senses. Sure enough, Samantha called Allison six months later to let her know her relationship with Max had ended.

Happy to hear she was ready to move on with her life, Allison and Samantha agreed to move into a condominium together. For the next year, they lived happily together, working during the week and going to clubs for drinks and a chance to meet Mr. Right on weekends. They were two 20-something-year-old women just doing their thing.

I was floored by what Allison told me next. A day or so after the burglary, she did an extensive "second-look" walk-through of the condominium to spot any additional details about the break-in that she hadn't reported to the police. She was too shaken at the time to notice exactly what was missing, except for a few personal items. And besides, it struck Allison as odd that burglars wouldn't take much of value after having to scale a back wall, jump on a landing, and then take a small leap into Samantha's bedroom just to get inside. Allison suspected they must have been looking for something specific, and that's when she started really digging throughout the home.

The first thing she did was rifle through Samantha's drawers and closet and the personal items in her desk. After two hours of searching she'd almost given up before finding a trunk Samantha kept stored under the bed. Fortunately, it was unlocked, and Allison wasted no time sifting through its items. It wasn't long before she found what she was looking for. Stuffed between two stacks of papers in a crumpled, yellow-clasp-bubble-envelope wrapped tightly with a rubber band was just over $32,000 in cash and a .357 Magnum handgun. Allison would later tell me the feeling of betrayal she'd experienced at that moment was even more profound than what she'd experienced growing up— she expected pain and suffering at home, but never expected it from Samantha.

Allison knew now that so much of what she believed about her friendship with Samantha was a lie. For the entire time they'd known each other, Samantha made it clear to Allison that, despite the challenges in her life, she was determined to be a woman who could stand on her own in every way. She wanted nothing to do with the illicit lifestyle of her birth parents, and though her foster families were caring people, she was determined to create in her own life a true place to call home.

Samantha's lifelong goal was to graduate from college and pursue a career in business, something no one in the history of her biological family had ever done. When she and Allison met, Samantha not only offered Allison her friendship but also virtually moved Allison into her foster parents' homes, letting Allison know that regardless of where Samantha was living, Allison was welcome to spend the night as often as she needed. Allison was impressed with Samantha's boldness and drive to succeed—it seemed they had plenty in common and could be a great support to each other.

But as Allison stared at the gun and pile of money in front of her, she realized Samantha had likely begun changing her mind about the kind of life she ultimately wanted. It now appeared that the very lifestyle she swore off had in fact become her way of life, and to Allison it felt like a deal breaker for their friendship. Allison's flood gates opened as she slowly started to put two and two together: Just months before, Allison happened to see a story on the six-o-clock news about a bank robbery near their condo. Now it made sense to Allison why Samantha ended her relationship with Max before the two women moved in together—the reason Max was no longer around was because he'd been jailed for armed robbery. And just like the first time, he was headed back to prison.

But Allison knew Max well enough to know he wasn't just going to forget about the money—no doubt it was his goons that came to retrieve the stolen money and firearm, which Allison was sure Max had no trouble convincing Samantha to "hold for him." The pile of money also explained Samantha's bags of new clothes and shoes from her recent shopping trips—the news segment reported that $40,000 had been stolen, but the amount Allison found was short of that amount. At that moment, Allison realized it was very likely Samantha was stealing from Max's till.

Allison told me she cried for weeks over the realization that the relationship she thought she had with her best friend was over. What she couldn't comprehend was how Samantha could be willing to compromise her lifelong goals and dreams for a lifestyle Samantha knew from experience would lead nowhere. Samantha knew the money had come from a robbery and that lives were at stake to get it and keep it, but getting her hands on the cash was more important. What's more, Samantha kept the stolen goods in a home she shared with Allison, an innocent bystander, and didn't think enough of their relationship not to bring blood money into the place where they should both be safe.

Allison told me that, had Samantha been any of the childhood friends who often befriended Allison for their own convenience, she would have packed up her things at once and never looked back. Allison may have just been learning at that time how to be her own best friend, but she had plenty of practice at dropping anyone who stood in the way of her future. But Samantha was different—she and Allison had a history. Allison had once believed she and Samantha would enjoy a lifelong pristine friendship that neither of them would want to blemish.

But Allison had to accept that Samantha's greed was more important. Samantha had taken money that put several people's lives in danger simply because they happened to be in the wrong place at the wrong time. And Allison might have been one of those lives had she not made a U-turn and decided to run an errand before coming home.

Lesson Twelve: Leave Ports of Call Behind

Thankfully, Allison listened to the advice she always gave Samantha. "When emotions are in play," she would say to her, "always do the opposite of what you feel like doing." Allison learned early on in their relationship that Samantha often had a hard time saying No to things that could hurt her, so Allison would share that advice with Samantha every chance she could. And Max was proof of the mistakes that Samantha could make if she let her emotions get the best of her.

So, Allison did "the opposite of what she felt like doing" and proceeded to sever contact with Samantha. She worked out an agreement with the landlord that let her out of the lease on the condo they rented together and began packing up her things. Allison walked away from this relationship and never looked back.

To this day, when Allison and I talk about Samantha, I see a great sadness come over Allison's face. But this time her sadness reflects not only the loss of her childhood friend, but Samantha's loss of herself. Samantha never did reach her lifelong goal of being a college graduate; she dropped out after the first year so she could spend time with Max. Max ended up being sentenced to 15 years in prison for his crimes, and Samantha gave up dreams of a professional career to be with a man who had no ability to be with her. Allison later heard through the grapevine that Samantha ended up in a small studio apartment in the same neighborhood her birth parents once lived, and became a single mother to a child who doesn't know his father.

It took a long time for Allison to stop feeling a tinge of guilt for walking away from Samantha, even though she knew in her heart it was the right decision. But I constantly remind her that hope is only powerful when the hope we have for ourselves is as strong as the hope others have for us. Regardless of how badly Allison wanted Samantha to succeed, the desire for personal success had to come from within Samantha. Despite Allison's efforts to show Samantha that there is great reward in standing for herself, Samantha didn't possess the capacity to love herself as much as Allison did. Allison was right to walk away before becoming co-dependent on the relationship and losing herself.

I often share the Dry Cleaner Story with clients who are struggling to trust their inner voices. I tell them that their intuition, or "sixth sense" is one of the most powerful weapons they have to protect themselves. I encourage them to use it and never second-guess what I call their "first mind." Regardless of what the outside voices say, I always remind my ladies to hear their own voice first. I remind them to make choices that let their light shine brightest and to avoid situations and people who seek to reduce their light to a mere flicker.

Eleven

FACING THE SQUALL

"Paid the cost to be the boss."

— JAMES BROWN

Of the many things in this world that bring me contentment, meeting women who embrace boldly all aspects of their lives is one of them. The courage to believe in ourselves fully and completely creates the valor needed to transform dreams into reality. When we women stand firm in who we are, we are unstoppable.

For years, women have asked me how I did it. How did I manage to overcome single-teenage motherhood, severe dyslexia and dysgraphia that made getting an education incredibly difficult, and a life destined for poverty to end up owning a thriving, million-dollar-business? I believe much of my success was a result of my uncompromising commitment to reaching my goals. Despite the bumps in the road, I worked hard and never let go of my creative vision of self-sufficiency.

The other thing I learned was not to define achievement through anyone else's eyes but my own. Especially during my housecleaning days, when the hours were long and the work sometimes backbreaking, I remained focused on the fact that I was doing what was needed to survive.

Housekeeping may not have been my end goal, but it was a step in the right direction. It fed me and my children, kept a roof over our head, and helped put a huge dent in my expensive cosmetology school tuition. I didn't allow anyone or anything to convince me that being a housekeeper meant I was at the bottom of the barrel. Instead, I chose my customers carefully and worked hard to provide them a service that was beyond anything they expected.

In grand, 10,000- and 15,000-square-foot Hillsborough mansions, I didn't just wash dishes and do laundry; I connected with my clients. When I helped them re-organize their closets, I also helped them re-assess their outlook on life. While showing them how to mix everyday products to remove stains that for years they hadn't been able to eliminate, I helped them eliminate emotional baggage and self-doubt. I didn't just scrub toilets and mop floors, I helped women scrub away negativity and mop up insecurities they believed held them back from realizing their greatest potential. I proved to the ladies of the houses that I was smart, determined, and trustworthy enough to hold their deepest secrets and provide sage advice when they needed it. I gained respect as a devoted member of their households and never once gave anyone a reason to refer to me as "just the maid."

To this day, I have a great love for the women I worked with—they shared their worlds with me while I helped them keep a handle on theirs. As I helped them polish brass fixtures and dust the trinkets and baubles they'd brought back from their European trips abroad, they shared stories of their travels that gave me a vision of life well beyond my current circumstance. Our economic environments may have been vastly different, but what we had in common was our dreams and hopes for the future. I knew that even if my life situation would not directly provide me the opportunity to become a leader in some of the companies they and their spouses oversaw, I could at least stand proud in their presence. Wearing my smock and holding sponges in my hands, I proudly jumped in on any discussions pertaining to business or leadership because I believed I was worthy of being there.

So, when I meet a woman who is afraid of embracing her unique path to success, I remind her that each day is a step toward discovering her personal genius. Though I knew even as a child I would not walk a "traditional" avenue toward success—and experienced great frustration, sadness, and anger because of it—I still learned to embrace my uniqueness.

I didn't understand until I was well into adulthood that as a dyslexic, my brain has great challenges deciphering the written word. But it is also hard-wired in such a way that I have a crystal-clear, unhindered perception of the world. Like many dyslexics before me—including billionaire financial genius Charles Schwab, notable actor Henry "The Fonz" Winkler, and Virgin Airlines founder Richard Branson—I had to come to terms with the fact that my "disorder" was truly my gift.

After years of struggling with reading, being bullied by students and teachers alike for not wanting to read aloud, and being called "lazy" and "stupid," I discovered after being officially diagnosed that my learning comes visually and spatially. I do not learn, as Allison has always said, "in a linear fashion." Thankfully, I had one special woman in my corner as a child to hold my hand and hold me up on the days when I felt particularly challenged. In fact, it was our shared feelings of being outcasts that brought Ms. Morgan and I together. She was a mentor at our local community center and one of the few White people that lived in my neighborhood. What I would later learn is that Ms. Morgan understood what it felt like to be bullied for being who she was—she was a proud educator of young kids and a volunteer tutor and counselor to kids who needed extra support. She was also a lesbian who lived with a lifelong partner she often referred to as her "cousin from Wyoming." Even in "free love San Francisco," Ms. Morgan was regarded as a great advisor to young minds as long as she was willing to "stay in the closet."

When I would see Ms. Morgan in and around the neighborhood, I'd greet her with a hug—each time, she'd ask me for what seemed like the millionth time why I didn't spend more time at the community center. Ms. Morgan would remind me often that I should "share my skills"—a leadership quality she saw in me early on—with other kids. "They could learn a lot from you," she'd say, trying to coax me into joining her as a student assistant. Each time she would ask I would come up with a different answer, hoping that sooner or later she would get tired of asking.

One day, Ms. Morgan stopped me as I was turning the corner to head up the hill toward home. We exchanged our usual hugs and asked each other about our day. But this time, Ms. Morgan didn't press me about joining her at the center—instead, she looked me straight in the eye and said she understood that "school-type activities weren't for everybody." She smiled as she spoke, but part of me was wondering what she meant.

Turns out, Ms. Morgan was having lunch with her partner at Lefty O'Doul's about a week earlier when she noticed me at the counter eating a meal and talking to a waitress she soon realized was my mother. Out of respect for a generation that had little tolerance for Ms. Morgan's sexual identity, she chose not to say hello to me or my mother, or introduce either of us to the woman she loved. Instead, she sat quietly, smiling proudly as she shared with her partner that I was one of the "good kids" from her neighborhood.

What Ms. Morgan also noticed was how I handled a request from a customer seated at the counter next to me. She had forgotten her glasses and asked for my help in clarifying a few key items on the menu. I smiled broadly and told the customer I was her waitresses' daughter and that I would have my mother come give her a hand. Like so many who suffer with silent disabilities, I focused not on what I couldn't do but on what I could, and one thing I knew how to do even as a little girl was to engage people and make them feel they mattered. This middle-aged woman and I talked for about 30 minutes; she shared stories about her life in San Francisco as a young woman in the 1940s and the generations of her family who had lived there. I happily shared stories about my family, proudly sharing that my Dad helped to paint some famous landmarks. The woman was impressed and said she looked forward to seeing me again anytime I'd come to visit my mother. To top things off, she told my mother to make sure that "your little girl gets this $5 tip for being so polite and thoughtful." Even as a young girl, I wished I could have helped this woman in the way she would have liked, but when I saw how happy I'd made her, I felt some level of vindication. I knew I was smart, but I just had a different way of expressing my intelligence—for me that situation was just another day of turning "can't" into "can."

When Ms. Morgan shared with me what she'd seen, she said it was because of that very scenario that she wanted my assistance at the center. She told me my unique ability to "think on my feet" and "think outside the box" was something she wanted all her students to do and she'd hoped I could lead by example. But, she told me, she also realized by watching my interaction with the customer at the restaurant that my ability to quickly evaluate a situation created other challenges that might make working as her student assistant difficult—there would likely be reading aloud from books of some kind and spelling out words onto paper, neither of which I could do easily. Even as a little girl I tried to always be strong, but that day I'd felt Ms. Morgan and I truly understood each other—we both knew the pain of having to keep a part of ourselves hidden from the world. As she hugged me and wiped from my face the few tears that escaped me, I told her that as determined as I was to succeed I didn't understand why I couldn't grasp what seemed like simple concepts for the other kids. And I was so tired of being called dumb when I knew I wasn't.

That's when Ms. Morgan reminded me I had plenty for which to be proud—she'd seen my "great communication skills in action" and told me I had the potential to be a great leader. Perhaps if Ms. Morgan and I had met during a more progressive time of life we'd have both had a better chance of being accepted for who we were. My teachers might have had a better understanding of dyslexia and would have been better equipped to help me in school. And Ms. Morgan could have lived "out and proud" in a world that celebrated all her qualities both as an educator and lesbian leader in the community.

Unfortunately, neither of us had the option of openly sharing our differences without fear of reprisal. It was the day Ms. Morgan "outed" that she knew about my secret disability that she also "outed" herself to me, explaining that she, too, had a secret that I was too young to understand but that one day she'd hoped to be able to tell the world. She said that she'd watched plenty of other people like her, who had shared their secret publicly, lose jobs, be disowned by their families, and even lose their lives. But her secret was a part of who she was and even if she couldn't share it she was not going to let anyone else define her. She told me that, like her, I was unique and that I should focus on being the best version of myself. I'm so thankful for that advice—Ms. Morgan's unique heart is the same heart that saw greatness in a differently-abled child when others could not.

These days, I am proud of the differently-abled mind that comes with being dyslexic. I embrace the idea that when I am presented with a problem to solve, meet a new person, or am faced with helping others overcome their specific challenges, I am immediately flooded with a massive amount of information about what's in front of me—I don't let the information overwhelm me; I instead use it to my advantage. I can visualize all the multi-dimensional aspects of that image or situation. I can clearly identify it, immediately rectify whatever inconsistencies exist, and make a judgment call about next steps, all at the same time. I'm able to see clearly what's been omitted and what adjustments need to be made, a task that might take a non-dyslexic minutes, hours, or even days to complete.

Within seconds, I have confirmed what is and what's needed for a positive outcome. All this information is processed in my brain at one time. It makes sense, then, that words on a page only create mental-time-lag and interrupt my complex thought process. By the time "readers" have reached the end of a sentence and have begun to comprehend and digest what they've read, I've already diagnosed, dissected, and decided what needs to be done.

Add that to my ability to assess, analyze, and interpret people in a split second, and the only thing reading becomes is an obstacle to my powerfully analytic mind. It's no wonder I'm able to create such poignant connections with people—I have my gifted, dyslexic brain to thank for that. If I had allowed myself to be victim to the labeling that comes with having a reading disorder, I'm sure my choices, and ultimately where I am today, would have been completely different.

In a world where the size of a paycheck is often the sole definition of achievement, it can be difficult to be the person who didn't go to college or work in the same fields as those who did. I can't count how many times in my formative years that I longed to be able to sit in board meetings with some of the greatest minds in business, but I knew that since my reading and writing skills were compromised, my road to success would take an alternative path. I'm grateful daily that I embraced that path, and I'm always willing to help someone else do the same.

Manage the Changing Tides

Collaborating with other artists who are blessed with an overwhelming drive to succeed always makes me feel proud that I chose hair replacement as a career. Not only do I get to live vicariously through their amazing creativity and ambition, but I also get to watch the public they serve benefit from their unique talents.

Jessica was one such woman. Though in my salon I'd only worked alone or with my daughter, I made an exception for Jessica. She was a stylist that understood the special bond between me and my clients, and I couldn't wait to watch her reach all her goals and aspirations.

For the first few months of working together, Jessica blew me away. She was smart, determined, and confident. A beautiful Latina with smooth, supple olive-brown skin, her jet black, long wavy tresses softly caressed the middle of her back when she walked. My clients constantly complemented her on her hair—after all, she had naturally what we all had to pay for. But she never once made anyone uncomfortable; as soon as a client complimented her, she'd give one right back, reminding everyone that we were all beautiful.

Her heartfelt connection with the clientele was genuine. Though not trained specifically to manage hair loss disorders, she had family members who'd struggled with thinning hair for years, and thus she came to work every day ready to induce hope in any client with whom she worked. Jessica knew the value of a full head of hair, and used laughter, kindness, and the latest styling tools and artistic designs to help women in need reemerge as themselves. Jessica was a woman truly after my own heart.

For months, working with Jessica was bliss. She followed my lead while effectively running her own independent business. She managed her own clients while staying in sync with the culture of the salon. Some clients suggested at one point she must have been an extended family member, given how well she fit in. Together we grew and prospered, and enjoyed each other's warmth along with the satisfaction of helping women heal and feel good about themselves.

About a year into our new endeavor, I came into work and found Jessica sobbing. She sat crossed leg in a chair with her head down in a corner of her private room. She explained to me through a tear-stained face that she would soon be leaving. I was floored. I didn't understand what could have brought on this decision. Jessica let on that this was her fourth attempt at "starting a business" and she felt once again that this venture was a failure. Completely dumbfounded, I asked her to explain why.

Red Sky in Morning

In the past, Jessica and her husband had owned several businesses together, including multiple franchises. The businesses helped pay the bills but didn't pay enough to be their only source of income—she hoped one day that would change, but she admitted she didn't have a clear business plan in place before she leapt. In the end, the ever-changing demands of running a franchise proved to be more than she could handle—her franchises eventually closed and left her credit in ruins.

Hoping to recoup some of her losses and still own a company that would bring in a sufficient income, Jessica reluctantly made plans to open her own salon. I listened intently as she explained. I understood well that sometimes we must crawl before we can walk—even though she was good at it, styling hair was far from being Jessica's choice of career, but she was committed to taking a first step into being the million-dollar business owner she believed she could be. Determined to make the salon a success, Jessica pounded the pavement to gain clients, advertised in local media, and worked hard to build a word-of-mouth referral list. It took some time, but eventually she saw her clientele move from a trickle to a flood and shortly thereafter was able to increase her staff of one to seven.

For a while, the business thrived. Eventually though, she started notic-ing that her clientele was dwindling. They stopped making their scheduled appointments, calling in the day or two before, saying they had to cancel. Others simply wouldn't schedule follow-up appointments after their services were completed, and when they did return for visits, they were several weeks, sometimes months past due. Jessica knew she was in trouble, but instead of methodically thinking her way through how to overcome the slump, she immediately began lowering her prices to accommodate her fickle clientele. This continued until current clients were asked to pay next to nothing for her services. And since her new referrals already had wind of the low prices, a price increase was not an option.

Jessica simply couldn't find a creative way to stay in business, and the store eventually shuttered. She admitted that being an independent contractor in my salon felt like a step down for her, and that as much as she appeared happy, she was extremely uncomfortable in my environment.

She told me there were days she hated to see me coming in, because she couldn't understand how I'd managed to stay in business when she'd made several attempts to do so and failed. "I should have been a millionaire by now," she'd admitted, squinting at the awards and accolades hanging on the walls that I'd earned over the years. I worked very hard to ignore the obvious frustration showing on her face, and instead tried to lend an ear to her unmistakable pain.

Jessica was one of the most talented and level-headed stylists I knew; she was determined, in my eyes, to be more than "just a hairdresser." I saw her as a partner, a business woman whose product happened to be hair. But what I came to realize is that Jessica wasn't willing to accept the many challenges that came with self-employment, and that troubled me.

I sat down in the corner with Jessica, held her hand, and assured her she was not alone. I let her know that despite my achievements, I, too, had struggled more times than she knew to keep my doors open, especially during the Great Recession of 2007. I understood clearly that when banks stopped lending to private citizens, and people were in danger of losing their homes, my business was going to be one of the first affected. I accepted this knowledge and just forged ahead. As a business owner, I didn't know one self-employed person who wasn't fiscally challenged during this time.

I explained that what we all had in common was that we didn't give up on our dreams, and we were willing to make whatever changes and/or sacrifices were required to keep moving forward. Furthermore, I reminded her, closing the doors to a business that's losing money doesn't mean you've given up your dreams: It just means that you're strong enough to do the right thing.

I applauded her for doing everything she could to make it work, but I also reminded her that if she wasn't careful, she could become her own worst enemy. She owed it to herself to learn from her mistakes and dismiss the negativity from her past, or it would prevent her from having a future.

I shared my housekeeping stories with her, and told her that I had to remind myself countless times that I was not a failure, even though there were many that tried often to convince me I was. In their eyes, I would never be able to come off the public assistance I once depended on to feed my children.

In their eyes, I could never be a sole proprietor of anything, and all I was ever going to be was "somebody's maid." I shared with her that I never allowed myself to think that way. I told her I knew cleaning houses was something I was good at because I could see structure and dimension through the eyes of an artist. Dirt, disorganization, and improper design of anything in the home were no match for me. This ability to visually and spatially compartmentalize an idea, thought, or object allowed me solve problems that a "maid" could not. To my clients, I was the person who engineered their home, rather than just cleaned it.

I shared with her that I would later apply that same visualization practice in designing my hair replacement prosthetics. Hair reconstruction uniquely addresses the specific hair-loss and/or scalp disorders of each client. Just like the way I approached cleaning a house, I knew no two heads were alike, and I could quickly problem-solve in each particular situation.

Even if two clients had the exact same diagnoses, I would need to provide two completely different solutions for their individual conditions. I could never assume that what worked today would work tomorrow, and therefore I was always prepared to create a solution from scratch. I knew I was an innovator—I had an uncanny ability to solve problems in unique ways and foster meaningful, lasting relationships. In this way, I found my genius.

I explained to Jessica that the moment we let people convince us that we are unworthy of achievement is the moment we fail ourselves. I told her that she should never allow others to dictate her value; often it's better to fire customers who are unable to appreciate your work than lower prices to accommodate them. Even during my darkest moments in my business, when I couldn't get a butt-in-seat to save my life, I refused to alter my work to fit the whim of those who didn't appreciate me anyway. I survived because I never let opinions of others be more valuable to me than my own.

I held Jessica and let her know I truly did understand her frustration. It's hard to be respected as a hairstylist—the general assumption is that we are not smart people and that we chose this line of work because we could not do anything else. Yet the stylists I've had the fortune of meeting in my career constantly remind me that nothing could be further from the truth. We chose this path because we are designers, creators, and visual architects, and we bring that unique set of skills to the men and women who seek our services.

Unfortunately, Jessica was so worn out by the challenges of running a business that she sabotaged her opportunity for surviving the downturn. She was so afraid of failing that fear itself became the deciding factor in her choices. So paralyzed was she at the thought of being defeated, that her mind simply could not be open to creating new ideas that could have been the shot in the arm her business needed. Surely, nothing in this life is guaranteed, but dedication to achieving our personal best makes the risk easier to endure. I've been forced to walk so many tightropes in my life, without a net, that taking risks is almost second nature to me. But I always kept my eye on the other end of the tightrope, and this helped me continue walking. I wanted Jessica to understand that, above all else, when we make allowances that are not within our best interest, we run the risk of being judged incapable and of little expertise.

Red Sky at Night

As I consoled Jessica and tried to give her the strength to hang on, I could hear Allison's voice in my head. "Pride goeth before a fall," her mother used to say to her, firing Bible scripture quotes at her like a heat-seeking missile. Biblical statements were used as a method of subjugation anytime Allison's mother felt Allison was showing signs of self-awareness or even a modicum of self-esteem. Either was a crime in her mother's mind, but despite her mother's intentions, Allison found a positive way of framing the quote.

Whenever she felt apprehensive in the face of a difficult choice, Allison would ask herself if it was her fear of a bruised ego that was causing her anxiety. If she determined that fear of failure, trepidation over being rejected, or the angst of possibly experiencing a complete downfall were to blame, she'd choose instead to put her ego aside and forge ahead. She knew that letting "pride" get in the way of a decision could keep her from embracing an opportunity that could change her life for the better.

I shared this idea with Jessica, letting her know that cowering in the face of a challenge or an attack on her abilities surrenders her personal power to those who already don't believe she is worthy of it. Whenever Jessica's immediate view of her situation didn't match her world vision, her initial, gut reaction was to start the process of walking away from what she'd created. But the truth is, she was afraid of having to face the executive responsibilities of being a commander-in-chief. Wanting to own a business, and being a successful business owner are two different things; this is a mistake many people make before grabbing the reigns of responsibility.

Jessica admitted her biggest fear was being a saleswoman of any kind, even if it was the thing most required for keeping her doors open. I remembered asking her on several occasions if she wanted to appear with me at media events or attend meetings that could help generate new business. I realize now that as gung-ho as she was to attend education workshops or participate in a salon event of any kind, no one was as apprehensive as she was to accompany me on new business endeavors. Now I realized why. Pitching herself and her business to anyone reminded Jessica that she believed deep-down she was unworthy of being in this position, and no amount of sales coaching or media training could change that.

I felt terrible for her. I knew that being able to think on her feet was a prerequisite for being in business. The moment we business owners clam up when meeting potential business partners or delivering our elevator pitches is the moment we can kiss our business goodbye. Selling ourselves is essential for gaining new customers, and I hurt that Jessica felt this was an obstacle she could not bring herself to overcome. I couldn't imagine being responsible for a franchise that cost several-thousand dollars a month to maintain and not having the courage to do what is needed to sustain it. Jessica would admit to me that she cowered even at the thought of having to sell to her own clients. Her "pride" and fear at the thought of being judged by anyone was a barrier to the survival of her business.

Lesson Thirteen: A Strong Captain Stays the Course

I tried to show Jessica during our conversation that anyone who has ever worked to have something in this life has tried and failed, some of us more than others. I reminded her that sometimes we can't discover our strengths until we discover our failures. Not only is it okay to fail, it can also be a rewarding experience to remain a humble servant to the uneven path before us. By reminding ourselves that our beginning is not our end, we can put aside our fears and open ourselves to opportunity. And by taking risks associated with that opportunity, we can embrace whatever life stage we're in. I shared with Jessica that one of the hardest things to do as a young woman was to put my pride aside so I could clean houses to feed myself and my children. Turns out, I was one of the best damn housekeepers around, and I made lasting relationships and a good living because of it.

Many assume that self-employment is easy because "you can make your own hours" or "be your own boss." But, in fact, business owners often work harder and longer than anyone else. I have more than my fair share of 16-hour workdays under my belt, and spending the night in my workplace was once so common I was lucky to ever see the inside of my home.

But no matter the stage of my business, I always kept in mind that all roads come to an end. That meant I could never sit back on my laurels when business was good, and I certainly couldn't throw in the towel when a challenge came my way. In fact, when business was at its best, I worked harder to formulate my next move. I know I'm only as good as the last hair-loss solution I've created. So, it was crucial to be better the next time.

I embrace equally the pros and cons, and tell myself daily that others respond to me based on how I carry myself, regardless of whether I'm having a good business day or a bad one. Nothing is one hundred percent consistent in the business world, but the one thing that can remain constant is how I choose to approach each day.

Jessica and I had a very long talk that day, and I hoped at the end of the conversation I had convinced her to stay and give it another try. But she soon revealed that several months earlier she had once again started lowering her prices. And once again, she had begun to lose clients. Just as before, reducing the cost of her services not only didn't keep her clientele on task for regular services, it likely contributed to them leaving altogether. My guess is that her current clients had the same issues as her previous ones: Watching their stylist lower her prices must mean she doesn't think she deserved any better.

Soon after, Jessica moved on. She eventually went to work doing clerical work for a private company. My hope for her is that whatever career path she's chosen, her dreams of being a success never die and that she can learn to make choices despite discomfort. I believe then she will overcome any stumbling block and move mountains on her journey toward happiness and prosperity. She will be a true shot-caller, and will finally learn to defeat any obstacle in her path. Jessica is an artist whose light shines brightest when she's doing work she loves, and by owning both her hopes and her fears, she can finally let her light lead the way.

Twelve

Caution: Piranha in Fresh Water

*"I know you've got a little life in you yet, I
know you've got a lot of strength left."*

– Kate Bush

I have great respect for people who do whatever it takes to achieve their goals. This is what I admired about Penelope. Penny, as I called her, came into my life during the early stages of my hairstyling career, seeking help for hair that had suddenly started to thin.

I was an-up-and-coming stylist working in a metropolitan salon. She was a 27-year-old corporate lawyer. Penny was determined to make sure her thinning hair and the varying bald patches that were starting to form didn't detract from her one objective—making partner by the age of 35. She'd heard through the grapevine that I was the person who could ensure her hair was a bridge, rather than a barrier, to achieving her goals. As I was for many clients, I became her confidant as well as her hair restoration professional, and she was always willing to help me understand any legal issues associated with running a business.

Penny was in the prime of her life when I met her, occupying a space in her career that she knew many envied. She graduated top of her class from a highly acclaimed law program and within months of joining the firm had a client list a mile long. She was a brilliant attorney, and I greatly valued any knowledge she was willing to share with me.

She'd come in for treatments and therapy services every six to eight weeks; during our time together she'd share with me some of her biggest case challenges and what she did to overcome the hurdles. Penny was a highly critical thinker. It was hard to stump her when it came to the law. Like me, she had a million different answers to a million different questions. I celebrated with her whenever she'd tell me she'd just won a huge case, and commiserated with her over her Herculean losses. Losses were a huge step backward for her and the firm, and she didn't want to give anyone a reason to think she was a less-than-stellar candidate for becoming partner.

We talked all the time about our future aspirations. Penny was determined to be a leader in her firm, and I was determined to one day have my own establishment that would cater to women like me and Penny, in privacy and comfort. Penny was always on my side, giving me advice about how best to move forward, and helping make sure I didn't miss any of the ins and outs of what I needed to do to succeed. I couldn't get enough and always looked forward to my next visits with her.

One day Penny came in while I was finishing with another client, so I didn't get the chance to greet her at the door with my usual hug. She sat in the waiting area while I tidied up and prepared for her service. When I finally did see her, the look on her face shocked me. Penny was always happy to see me, so anything other than a huge grin on her face caused me worry. What I was seeing was clear sadness, frustration, and a whole lot of anger. I'd hoped to God it had nothing to do with her hair.

I rushed her to my chair to see what was going on. Penny proceeded to explain that she felt like her life was falling apart.

I was dumbfounded. Even with the small amount I knew about Penny's life, I felt certain she was one of my few clients who was working toward "having it all." She was blessed with an amazing mind, was earning an exceptionally high salary working for a firm she'd had her eye on since leaving law school, and had recently bought a house in an upscale neighborhood. She was also planning her dream wedding to a man she'd known most of her life. I was so proud of her accomplishments; to me she was a trailblazer for other women.

I asked her to explain. Her sadness turned to stoicism. I could tell she was doing her best to steel herself against whatever bad news she was about to reveal. She took a cleansing breath, then slowly let on that her fiancé was cheating on her. After years together and a lifetime of history with this man, this was more than she could bear. And that wasn't all. She said there were major financial problems between them that could end up affecting her entire career. Now it was my turn to take a cleansing breath.

Swimming in Shark-Infested Waters

Penny explained that the night before, she was at a company meeting with several of the partners. They had recently tapped her to work a huge case, confident that she could close the deal and make the firm a ton of money. There was a bonus in it for her, too, so naturally Penny wanted to assure the partners they had nothing to worry about.

To make a good impression, she offered to pick up the check. Quickly adding up the alcohol and meal cost in her head, Penny knew she was going to have to dig deep to cover this one; the partners knew how to entertain well, and Penny knew to be prepared. When the over-$2,000 check arrived at the table, she reached for it before anyone else, letting her bosses know it was the least she could do in exchange for them putting her front-and-center on this huge case. Smiling, she gladly slid her platinum American Express in the card slot and continued chatting with the partners as she finished her glass of wine.

She said she was having such a good time that what she saw next almost didn't register. She glanced nonchalantly across the room and saw a man she thought might have been her fiancé. Couldn't be, she thought. He's not even in town; at least that's what he'd told her the previous week when he called to cancel a dinner date. He said he was leaving on business, but would call her as soon as he returned. Penny didn't give it a second thought—they were both hard-working young, urban professionals. Duty called.

She turned her head and looked again, trying to make sure the wine wasn't confusing what she saw. This time, she was sure it was him, sitting at a table with a beautiful, slender, blond-haired woman she'd never seen before. As a top attorney, Penny had one of the best poker faces I'd ever seen, so of course she didn't let on that anything was wrong. But inside, she felt like someone had just punched her in the stomach. All at once she was embarrassed, hurt, and distraught, and it took everything she had to keep a straight face in front of her bosses. All she wanted to do was get the check and get out of there. Once she was free of the partners, she could better focus on how to deal with this nightmare.

The check came back to the table a few minutes later. As Penny readied herself to sign the receipt, the waiter leaned in and told her the credit card was declined. Good thing Penny was a brown-skinned, African-American woman, or the partners would have immediately seen the red flush rising in her face. She politely offered the waiter another card, saying there must be a mix-up. Penny waited a few more moments for him to return with a new receipt. This card, too, was declined.

Penny was now absolutely fit to be tied. "Already I'm a Black woman trying to make an immaculate impression," she told me as I was treating her. "I have enough to worry about without everyone thinking I don't deserve to manage a million-dollar contract because I'm not even capable of keeping my own credit intact." She caught one of the partners giving her a defiant side-eye as she fumbled with her wallet; after watching two of her credit cards decline, they were starting to doubt her financial stability. Penny knew she had one more shot before one of them reached for their billfold to solve this debacle.

That's when she yanked out the only other card that could support this kind of transaction, but it was the last card she thought she'd ever have to use. It was the debit card linked to the checking account she'd opened to save for her wedding, and thankfully it had a $5,000 spending limit. Confident there shouldn't be any problem whatsoever with this card, she handed it over. Sure enough, the waiter came back with the receipt a few minutes later and proudly handed her the card wallet for her signature. Penny breathed a huge sigh of relief, but was reeling at having to spend $2,000-plus from an account she'd opened solely for wedding expenses. There was no point in having the damn account if she was going to have to spend the funds on everything but the wedding.

As she signed, she politely explained to her colleagues that she figured the initial mishap was the bank activating some kind of card protection. Whatever the issue, she assured the partners she'd work it out and it wouldn't be a problem again. Thankfully all turned out well and she managed to maintain favor with the partners.

When she got home that night, she started investigating immediately. She dialed the credit companies as fast as she could, tapping her fingers on her desk rapidly as she waited for what seemed like a lifetime for a representative to come to the phone. She wanted to know why on Earth, as a woman with an excellent credit record, extensive credit line, and years of on-time balance payoffs, her cards were being declined. And that's when the shit hit the fan. She discovered over $50,000 worth of merchandise had been charged to her American Express cards, and additional purchases were now being flagged.

Once she got wind of the items on the statement, it only took a second to put two and two together. Her fiancé had purchased expensive jewelry, plane tickets, lingerie, and clothes, none of which she had received. She realized immediately that the woman sitting in the restaurant must have been the beneficiary of the merchandise. At that moment, she said, it took every bit of restraint she had to keep from marching back to that restaurant and putting one solid bullet right between the eyes of that cheating son-of-a-bitch. Her fiancé had managed to damn-near cost her the opportunity of her career and damage her personal credit so badly she'd be lucky if she had anything left. All so his triflin' ass could impress some woman on Penny's dime.

The more she researched, the more she found. This dude had hustled over $200,000 from various credit cards, including accounts she didn't even know she had. Apparently, he was making the minimum required payments to keep the accounts in good standing, so the credit card companies assumed these were her accounts. So now, on top of everything else, she was involved in an identity-theft case—even if she was the victim, having a legal case of any kind didn't bode well for the perfect image she was working so hard to maintain.

Setting Sail in a Tsunami

When Penny confronted her fiancé, he had no choice but to come clean—she threatened him with prosecution if he didn't disclose all the details. After waffling back and forth he finally admitted everything. The worst part was he said he loved her and didn't want to hurt her, but recently had begun feeling like a second fiddle to her "fancy dinners, long work hours, and her 'bonding' time with the partners." Penny's fiancé was a marketing executive but she was clearly the breadwinner—this, along with her clear commitment to becoming partner, was just too much for him. In coming clean about the money, he also admitted to several affairs and made it clear he had no intention of being faithful to her anymore.

Penny was in shock upon realizing she was losing what she and her fiancé had been building together. Her fiancé was a huge part of the image Penny worked hard to portray—as the perfect likeness of the All-American male, he was her ticket to a social upgrade. Being the wife of this blue-blooded, WASP arm candy was the final ornament she needed to dress up her perfect persona, even if she was already a powerful attorney in her own right. So the shock of knowing he'd traded Penny in for another "prized trophy" who simply appeared to be a more publicly acceptable version of herself was more than she could bear. Despite her obvious intelligence, superior occupation, and well-packaged appearance, Penny realized she just wasn't good enough.

Most troubling for her was how hard she'd worked to avoid the relationship pitfalls of her peers. This was a man she'd known since they were kids, and she knew he was of the right "stock." He came from a long line of wealthy, successful businessmen, and his family was well-known in the town where they were both raised. She was even smart enough to begin drawing up a prenuptial agreement but in her heart felt it wouldn't be necessary.

Penny did all she could to keep up the air of perfection. She glowed with self-confidence when she wore her bespoke black or navy-blue power suits, all made in the finest gabardine wool with Joan-Crawford-inspired shoulder pads that underscored her already powerful demeanor. She coupled her tailored wardrobe with gossamer high-collared, long-sleeved silk-white blouses buttoned to the top, typically accented with pearls or a tie. Both her male and female colleagues knew to take her seriously.

And now that she was my client, no one was the wiser that her perfectly cut, mid-'80s power bob was really a hair prosthetic I'd designed for her—Penny could not afford a blemish of any kind, personally or professionally. But at this moment, in her mind, the groundwork for dismissal from her job, upcoming marriage, and in her opinion, her entire life, was laid.

I held my lovely Penny as she cried tears of pure desperation, realizing everything she'd been groomed to be was falling apart. She couldn't imagine that, after being raised in a prominent family from the South, after years of etiquette training for her presentation as a debutante, after getting into the right university and law school and having a family name that could open doors anywhere, she was failing. As I had done with so many women before her, I tried to comfort her and let her know this wasn't the end. But inside, I knew that in her mind, it was.

At that moment, I remembered Penny had once told me her lifelong dream was to be a high-end handbag and jewelry designer. She loved the high-fashion designs that perfectly accessorized her authoritative look, and she secretly coveted the opportunity to be a major player in the fashion industry. She envisioned her couture label at high-end department stores and exclusive boutiques. I couldn't help but wonder where she'd be now if she had chosen to pursue her true interest. She wouldn't have been any less smart, any less talented, or any less driven. Perhaps that same drive would have allowed her to realize the dreams she'd put on hold to follow what was in her mind a more realistic career.

I sighed deeply as I held her, my superwoman who was struggling to overcome her personal kryptonite battle. Penny reminded me of so many other corporate professionals I'd come to know as I was building my career. I was in awe of their dedication and commitment; they worked long hours and weekends, traveled extensively, and worked hard to foster their personal relationships with the little time they had left. Some days Penny was so exhausted from her workday that she could barely keep her eyes open by the time she'd come to see me.

Anyone willing to yield that kind of commitment to an organization had my complete respect. I admired those who swore by their corporate packages and handed out embossed business cards with VP titles like they were a badge of honor. Penny and her colleagues lived for the martini lunches, private chauffeurs, and the paychecks that came with huge bonuses and great retirement packages.

I applauded them for being exactly where they'd wanted to be. Watching Penny and others like her gave me a glimpse of what my life might have been like if I'd had the opportunity to pursue a traditional career in business. I loved listening to their company anecdotes and enjoyed providing commentary about business issues. I commended them all for their accomplishments and loved participating in this part of their lives.

What many of them also let on to me in private was that they weren't nearly as content with their lifestyles as they appeared to be. One of the gifts for which I am most grateful is that I am loyal to those with whom I'm connected. I take pride in knowing I will never betray the deepest secrets shared with me, and it's for this reason some of my corporate executives confessed to me time and again how truly unhappy they were with the lives they'd created. Trying to hold back the tears, they'd admit they'd signed up for the corporate career, suburban home, and two-point-five kids only because that's what they were groomed to do. Some told me that if it weren't for the money, they would've split the scene a long time ago. Each of them in their own way expressed regret over their choices. But they were so entrenched in the world they'd built that it seemed almost impossible to find a way out.

This was the reason Penny was sobbing so uncontrollably. She felt completely stuck in a career that was only reasonably fulfilling, and now everything she'd built that might have seemed to make her choices worthwhile was crumbling. Penny was fearful of being labeled a failure by her peers; she'd run so far on her company fast track that she felt there was no end in sight. What was once her open roadway with infinite possibilities had now morphed into a tunnel with no light at the end, and she was feeling completely claustrophobic.

Outsmarting the Hurricane

I could only hold Penny's hand and tell her there was still time. It's never too late to re-invent and re-emerge, and as brilliant a business mind as Penny possessed, I knew she had the potential. But I also knew somewhere in her mind she was locked into the idea that this lawyering way of life was her only means of achieving success. Not because she craved being an amazing lawyer, but because she craved what the title and its trappings brought her.

When Penny told people she was an attorney, they immediately took notice of everything she said and granted her their automatic approval. The thought of having to tell people she was "only" a handbag and jewelry designer, regardless of the level of success she may have achieved, would have been more than she could take. I've had the honor of telling people for years that I am a hair replacement professional. I can only imagine where I'd be today if I'd believed this profession to be beneath me, and instead committed myself to years in a career that returned rewards only others deemed appropriate.

Throughout the many discussions we'd had about her life as lawyer, I did my best to encourage Penny to find a way to incorporate her love for design into her life. Of course, after years of education, training, and working in the field of law just to be able to get a foot in the door of her current firm, I never expected her to drop everything and head to the nearest craft store. But I wanted her to think long and hard about creative ways to pursue her passion and still exercise her love for jurisprudence. She was young and had a full life ahead of her. Sure, she might be faced with making some adjustments, but she'd be fundamentally happy. Instead, here she was, searching for herself, afraid that her true identity was so hidden behind the suit that it could never be found.

Lesson Fourteen: Sail Through Surprises with an Open Mind

Whenever I'm asked for career advice from anyone, I remind them that there is no one right way to be a success. Particularly for my ladies like Penny, who've been groomed since childhood to believe there is only one direction to take. I encourage all people to spread their wings and spend some time discovering what makes them happy. Choosing a career solely based on money can be detrimental—eventually we must come face-to-face with the life choices we've made and we can only hope there are no regrets.

Allison once told me about the career choice she was almost forced into. Despite having dyscalculia and zero aptitude for math and science, she was pushed to find work as a computer programmer or engineer, just as her three older siblings had done. Each time she brought up the idea of working in a non-scientific field she was ridiculed: The phrase "soft scientist"—used to poke fun at her decision to pursue a career in the liberal arts—had a special place in her family's lexicon. But Allison pressed ahead to carve out the future she wanted, even it meant working in a field that yielded considerably less money than those of her family members. Given all the professional and personal success she's had thus far, I'd say it was one of the best choices she's ever made.

I, too, sometimes still get the "just a hairdresser" look from people. There are those who will always be convinced that stylists are nothing but simple-minded fools with a comb and shears whose only job is to play around on a canvas of hair. To them, our line of work is a consolation prize rather than a serious choice of career. At least that's what they would think until they'd see me climb into my Lamborghini or S-Class Mercedes, two of the several cars I purchased as my hairstyling career began to prosper. These onlookers could tell I wasn't in finance or computer science, and when I'd let on that my work was in hair, they were stunned. "Maybe I should have gone into hair," they'd say, realizing at that moment that hairstyling had the potential to be lucrative.

What they may never appreciate is that becoming a success in this multi-billion-dollar-a-year market takes a ton of business acumen and an even greater amount of street smarts. On top of the knowledge required to keep a retail space profitable year after year (or several at a time), stylists are therapists and healers. Particularly for those of us who serve special-needs clients, we deal at any given time with our clients' medical, physical, mental, and emotional issues each time we sit them in our chairs. For many people, we are their most trusted confidantes. We are privy to intimate details about their lives—some of which their family members may not be aware. We have changed entire lives in the time it takes to do a haircut or color. This line of work is not for people who want "an easy job," or whose only interest in becoming a hair specialist is because they see dollar signs.

Penny is now in her late fifties, and is still working at the prestigious law firm of which she worked so hard to become a member. She's one of only two female, majority-equity partners, and is considered one of the best attorneys in the industry. We still laugh when she comes in for her appointments, and she's resigned herself to knowing that this is her life. A year after her fiancé left, Penny was back in the financial black; she used her wits, her legal skills, and her close network of friends to help get back on her feet.

Today she's a rich woman by average standards; she'll be able to retire in a few years without financial worry. But I still see the sense of longing in her eyes when she watches me design for my clients. I know that her heart still aches for the opportunity to be an artist. But after years in the corporate battlefield, the passion she once had to pursue that dream, even on a part-time basis, is no longer there. Time has passed. She's aged, and she's tired. She knows her time has come and gone, and so we use our time together now to celebrate the incredible accomplishments she's made as an amazing legal counselor.

I've watched Penny grow up, and I'm thankful each day that even if that meant giving up on her personal dreams, she did what she had to do for herself. Along the way she triumphed over a financial blow that could have ended her career, survived the breakup with the only person she ever considered her life-partner, and still managed to become the head of a coveted legal organization. Sometimes we simply must take the path that's laid for us, because we know fighting against it could result in an even bigger battle.

In Penny's case, her genius was in knowing what she was good at, and she wasn't afraid to make the sacrifices required to realize her own definition of success. Even if in the beginning she did exactly as she was told and followed the path that was laid for her by her family, it turned out that Penny loved the law. She was good at it, and it gave her the opportunity to be financially secure. Maybe she'll find it one day in her heart to somehow pursue her craving for art, and she can thank her years of hard work as a corporate attorney for the financial means to do so.

Sometimes these unexpected twists in our lives deliver surprises we could never see coming. When that happens, it's up to us to be open to the opportunities those surprises bring about. I would never have known that I had such amazing sales and people skills had I been afraid to veer slightly off course into housekeeping. It wasn't my first choice of career by any means. But having the courage to sell my ideas to the heads of these grand homes gave me the financial stability I needed when longed-for success came calling. Penny followed her gut, even if meant her dream job had to take a back seat. She listened to her inner voice, and it turned out to be the best thing for her. Sometimes our She-Compass navigates a course with which we may be unfamiliar, but if we persist honestly toward discovering our true selves, we'll ultimately end up heading in the right direction.

Thirteen

WEATHERING THE STORM

*"Someday a loving hand will be laid upon our shoulder
and this brief message will be given: Come home."*

— BILLY GRAHAM

The stories my ladies have shared with me over the years have brought me joy and sadness, happiness and grief. But I keep listening, knowing that just being accessible to people as they navigate their world can make all the difference between them swimming comfortably in uncharted waters and sinking miserably. To be courageous, we must first feel encouraged; I will continue to use the wisdom I've gained through my experiences to help women everywhere take full ownership of their life's journeys.

My years of service to women in need reminds me daily that it can take a tremendous amount of strength to be a human being. I've had the honor for years to be a passenger on many of their journeys and have witnessed firsthand their daily battles with physical illness and the related hair loss conditions it brings. The bravery it takes to face boldly ominous life-threatening opponents makes me know my clients are nothing short of heroic. For some of my special ladies, simply being able to feel visible is a triumph unto itself. They are simply struggling to survive, and in so doing teach many of us how to live fully.

Courageous Captains Lead by Example

As a hair loss survivor, I understand all too well what it is to feel like an obstacle to be avoided, a mistake to be overlooked. Amy felt the same way, she told me, the day she showed up in my salon. It was early-October and I remember the yellow floral-patterned sundress she'd worn to survive the heat of this Indian Summer day. Her gold, strappy flat sandals showed off her freshly pedicured toenails.

As she stood in the doorway, I could see clearly the way-too-yellow, ill-fitting synthetic wig that was supposed to pass for her natural blond hair. In my mind I applauded her effort to cover the obvious patches of her thinning blond-white hair peeking through the poorly made hairpiece. My trained eye also quickly caught the scars on her scalp—at that moment, I knew instantly why she was here and I knew I could help solve her problem.

I tried to reach in for a hug as I met Amy's beautiful blue eyes, but instead of looking right at me she turned her head to the direction of my voice and smiled over my shoulder, as if to gauge the position in which I must be standing. As she attempted to reciprocate the hug, that's when I noticed her boyfriend gently coming up behind her and nudging her into my direction. She hugged me back tightly, and the realization that she'd done her very best to cover up her hair loss without being able to see what she was doing made me even prouder to have her as my client. I was honored to help care for Amy and witness her embrace of life, despite being blind and, as I would come to soon learn, despite suffering from an auto-immune disease that caused her severe physical pain.

I held her hand in mine as I slowly guided her into the building. We sat and talked for a while and I listened closely as she shared with me how she lost her sight. As a child, Amy was one of a few survivors of a car accident caused by a drunk driver—this was the second DUI the driver had received in less than six months, and his decision to drive that night with a blood alcohol level three times the legal limit took several lives. Two of those lives were those of Amy's parents. She spent her fifth birthday in a hospital trying to survive life-threatening broken bones and internal injuries. The doctors treating her had little hope she would make it, so when she emerged from her battle with the worst of her injuries being blindness, her surviving family members felt their prayers had been answered. Somehow Amy survived, but the damage done to her body was permanent. She suffered a lifetime of physical pain along with battling an autoimmune disorder that developed in her early teens. She was on every conceivable medication just to have some semblance of a "normal" life, and it was the hair loss side effects of that medication that brought her to me. At this point in her life, she explained, she didn't know how much of her life she had left, but she wanted to enjoy it while she still had it. She wanted to look and feel her best always because she knew tomorrow was not promised.

I listened as she explained more about her illness, creating mental designs in my head as I examined her scalp and noted the details of her medical history. We worked together to create the hair of her dreams and at each follow-up visit I looked forward to hearing about the compliments she received. We spent the next several months together in a constant state of laughter. She'd laugh at my silly Diana Ross impressions, and I'd laugh at the hilarious jokes she and her boyfriend would tell me as I worked.

Amy was a natural beauty and her kindness and love for life made her even more beautiful. Her visits with me were no more than an hour at a time, but she made it clear that time was only to be spent talking about things that made her happy. Though I assured her this was a safe space to share her concerns about anything, she still chose not to talk about her troubles—she told me that she was happy as long as she could "keep this beautiful hair on my head," and that when she was with me that was the only thing on which she wanted to focus. So that's what we did. Until one day, we didn't.

Final Destination

In the middle of a very busy Saturday, about two years after Amy and I had been working together, I received an unexpected visit from Amy's boyfriend. At first, seeing him alone didn't shock me; he took great care of Amy, and I'd assumed he was coming by to talk about her hair or grab a few hair products that needed replenishing.

I opened the door, leaned in to give him a quick hug, and that's when I noticed the tears streaming down his face. I held onto the doorframe and steeled myself—I knew this day was coming but I'd hoped it wouldn't be this soon. Amy's boyfriend slowly explained that Amy had experienced cardiac arrest during the previous night and died in her sleep. Her body had finally succumbed to its injuries, and he wanted to come by in person to tell me. The raw emotions flooded me—I work with women every day who are facing their mortality and this part never gets easier. I am an integral part of my ladies' lives, and when one of those lives is lost, a part of me is lost, too. All I could do was hold Amy's boyfriend and try to stay focused on the myriad women still in my salon who needed my help. So many times, I've held fathers, brothers, husbands, sons, and boyfriends as though they are my own family whenever their female family members are in pain. Above all else, I want them to know how much I love the women they love.

Amy's boyfriend slowly pulled away from me a moment later and took a second to compose himself while I held his hand. He stared at the ground as he spoke softly, saying he wanted to ask me something very important and that was another reason he wanted to come see me in person. He told me that no one, other than he and Amy, knew Amy wore any kind of hair prosthetic. He explained that Amy's hair meant the world to her and was one of the biggest reasons for her daily happiness. Her hair was the one thing that made her feel complete, and that even though she couldn't physically see it, the compliments she received daily from family and friends made her know she was beautiful.

He explained that she would never want anyone to have the opportunity to reduce her hair to "just a wig," and especially now that she was gone, he wanted everyone to remember her just as she was. His sweet brown eyes looked up at me at that moment, begging for help. What he didn't realize was that I already knew what he wanted—I've always said that my ladies are the same to me, whether they are walking in their bodies or their souls are at permanent rest. Before he could get the words out, I assured Amy's boyfriend I would be there for Amy and would make sure she was as beautiful in death as she was in life.

A Radiant Sunset

Knowing, loving, and being able to help Amy was one of the proudest moments of my career. I met with Amy's boyfriend privately at the funeral home and proceeded to do what I do best—I gave my incredibly strong, determined, and tenacious client back the crowning glory that had eluded her. As I placed her beautiful head into position and proceeded to spray, curl, tuck, and pin her lovely golden locks into place, I reminded myself of the importance of always having the moral courage to rise to the highest challenges of being human. Of all the obstacles Amy faced daily, facing death was her biggest showdown. She knew her time on Earth would quite possibly be ending sooner than she'd hoped, and she made the choice to always focus on the positive, despite the imminent future that lay ahead.

Amy never talked about what it must have been like to wake every day with great challenges—she couldn't take in visually the picturesque colors of a season's foliage or enjoy without excruciating pain a quiet walk in the park. She lost the chance early on to experience the loving arms of her mother and the sage advice of her father. She never complained about not being able to see the eyes of the man who never missed our appointments and who always made sure her hair was perfectly combed and her lipstick perfectly applied. And she never complained about the time she undoubtedly knew wasn't on her side, as the disease that attacked her bones and central nervous system continued to progress.

Amy focused instead on finding the joy in each moment. With the time she had left in this world her only goal was to be the best person she could to herself and to those whom she would soon leave behind. Amy always told me that just because she couldn't see the roses didn't mean she couldn't smell them. No matter how hard I tried to encourage Amy to open up about whatever troubled her, she refused to use what little time she had left to focus on her pain. She spent all our time together embracing the present and wanted only to look toward a future of contentment. Amy held tight to her She-Compass, and used it every moment of every day to guide her soul toward a sea of fulfillment.

I will always remember Amy as a teaching soul—her only mission was to show others how to be truly cognizant of who they are. Just by virtue of being, she taught everyone with whom she came into contact how to be better to themselves and others. She wanted only to positively affect the world around her, and she lit up the lives of those she touched like a lighthouse on a darkened sea. Amy wanted nothing more than to know she'd lived her life fully, and she carried this thought with her as her life-vessel made its way to the dock that would be her final destination. Amy's body may now be at rest, but her unsinkable soul will sail the seven seas forever. I often think that if more of us listened to our She-Compass as much as Amy did hers, we would once and for all find our true spirit and become completely fulfilled.

Lesson Fifteen: Never Give Up the Ship

I've said to Allison for years that we find true love when we truly learn to love ourselves. I stand with my sisters, who are tenaciously traveling life's oceans and searching to understand and embrace their uniquely crafted vessels. I know oceans are vast, their depths ample, and their currents strong. But when we each recognize our own power, we can overcome the seas' highest waves with determination and fearlessness.

I encourage my sisters to be totally, completely, and authentically themselves. I know that there is genius in tenacity, and I stand with my sisters who are not afraid to challenge or be challenged. I celebrate women who are kind to those in need but forbid the underestimation of their power. I am comforted by women who embrace life's obstacles with a humble heart yet are also brave soldiers in the fight to protect themselves and those they love. I stand with my sisters whose journey is long and those whose pilgrimages are ending. A friend in need is a friend indeed, and I am honored to be a skipper and co-captain to my sisters traveling in challenged waterways and rivers of complexity. Love is a powerful tool, and even in the darkest conditions, it's the instrument that untangles the most complicated predicaments. My wish for my sisters of the world is that we all find our She-Compass, the great love that resides in all of us. May we use it to recognize, embrace, and truly own the enormity of our humanity, and may we ultimately use it to inspire a great love in others.

The End